MADIBA
A TO Z

MADIBA
A TO Z

THE MANY FACES OF NELSON MANDELA

DANNY SCHECHTER

Seven Stories Press
NEW YORK

Seven Stories Press
140 Watts Street
New York, NY 10013
www.sevenstories.com

College professors and middle and high school teachers may order free examination copies of Seven Stories Press titles. To order, visit www.sevenstories.com/textbook or send a fax on school letterhead to (212) 226-1411.

Book design by Jon Gilbert

Frontis: A classic portrait of Nelson Mandela's radiant smile taken after he left office, with an AIDS awareness pin on his shirt. Courtesy of Mandela Centre of Memory. Photo by Matthew Willman.

Library of Congress Cataloging-in-Publication Data
Schechter, Danny.
 Madiba A-Z : the many faces of Nelson Mandela / Danny Schechter. -- A Seven Stories Press First edition.
    pages cm
 Includes index.
 ISBN 978-1-60980-557-9 (pbk.)
 ISBN 978-1-60980-559-3 (hc.)
 1. Mandela, Nelson, 1918- 2. Presidents--South Africa--Biography.
 3. Political prisoners--South Africa--Biography. I. Title. II. Title:
Many faces of Nelson Mandela.
 DT1974.S35 2013
 968.06'5092--dc23
 [B]
                              2013033539

Printed in the United States

9 8 7 6 5 4 3 2 1

For the freedom fighters who died and the freedom fighters
who fight on after the liberation.

CONTENTS

FOREWORD

Anant Singh

producer, *Mandela: Long Walk To Freedom*

AT OUR Videovision Offices in Durban, South Africa, there are twelve large color photos honoring Nelson Mandela, each offering a different insight into the man our country knows by his clan name, Madiba, and a leader I have been fortunate to know as a friend.

In one picture he is smiling, even guffawing, laughing aloud in a way that would seem to contradict the more formal images in the official portraits. In another, we just see the back of his head as he lectures a group of schoolboys, mostly white, all rapt attention. In still another, there is a wistful picture of his then-wife Winnie at the peak of her beauty and militancy staring off next to a photo of a smiling younger and dapper Nelson in a characteristic 1950s pose wearing a smart suit with a distinctive hairstyle of the time.

Each one of the twelve photos shows a different face of the man who was once the world's most famous political prisoner, but who, because of the apartheid regime's edict that his image be banned, for many years we couldn't see. Mandela himself was often reluctant to let his enemies—or even his friends—into his emotional life. Because of the discipline it took for him to survive the years of brutal imprisonment, he was forced to go "inside" in order for his thoughts and dreams to survive.

FOR THE last sixteen years, I have been obsessed with one idea: to bring Mandela's story to the big screen, to popularize and memorialize his remarkable journey, the story he tells in his autobiography, *Long Walk to Freedom*, first written behind bars, and then completed after his release from prison decades later. I wanted to offer the world a film we could be proud of, one that would do justice to what Madiba has given to our country and the world.

I was blessed when he awarded us the rights to his story, insisting that South Africans be the ones to tell this uniquely South African story, even as he wondered at first whether anyone would be interested in seeing a movie of his life. Such was his humility and faith.

Making the movie became a long walk in itself. I never expected it to take so long. But when you do something as complex as *Long Walk*, and do it in a way that is a fitting tribute and honest account of an amazing life, it can't be rushed. It has been an uphill battle. There have probably been fifty-five drafts of the screenplay over a period of fifteen years. As is common in making films of this scale, one piece comes in, two pieces fall out, another two pieces come in, one piece falls out.

Over time we assembled a team better than any we could have hoped for when we were starting out, and together we created a movie that has turned out better than we ever hoped it would.

We have dedicated ourselves to telling this story in a way that is informative and entertaining, that doesn't feel like a documentary but a drama, and can rivet moviegoers who already know something about Mandela's courage and commitment but also are open to learning more about his suffering and sacrifice. I was fortunate in having William Nicholson write the screenplay. He worked with me on *Sarafina!*, and also won recognition for his work on *Gladiator* and *Les Misérables*, to cite but two outstanding films from his impressive body of work.

Our first task was to immerse ourselves in learning every detail we could about Mandela's long life. We were fortunate to have his formidable best-selling autobiography as our underlying work. We consulted the vast library of other books and films about him and consulted with the people who knew him best. We enjoyed the full cooperation of the Nelson Mandela Centre of Memory that he established, with its vast archive of documents and data. We were also fortunate to have had Ahmed "Kathy" Kathrada, a close friend and confidante of Madiba who spent twenty-six years in prison with Madiba, guide us through the process. Kathy has been a staunch supporter of the project throughout the sixteen years, providing encouragement, motivation, and advice.

We left few stones unturned in this research effort over the years. It was as if we were acting as scholars and scavengers at the same time—tunneling into the details (and sometimes the dirt) to find a hook for how best to tell the story. We didn't want to end up with a PhD thesis but rather to find the path through the conflicts, contours, and contradictions of his life, and then to bring that story "alive" in a film that would be believable and exciting to watch.

We believe we have achieved what at times has felt like an impossible goal, thanks to the moving and textured performances of Idris Elba as Mandela, and Naomie Harris as his former wife Winnie. We sought out younger stars with international followings so that the film could find an audience, especially with younger people around the world. We attracted the involvement of top South African actors as well, and used thousands of extras, ingenious costumers, talented makeup and prosthetic teams, and a skilled production designer to create the look of a deeply lived life stretching from the 1920s to 1994.

Justin Chadwick, a young and passionate director of quality films like *The Other Boleyn Girl* and *The First Grader*, took charge of a film that required more than eighty days of shooting all over South Africa, often on the original locations. It was an expensive undertaking but well worth it as the audience will see.

INEVITABLY, in filmmaking, you have to take creative license, compress characters, leave out events, and invent ways to tell the story that will sustain interest. I believe our fellow Long Walkers have done that.

Remember that during Madiba's long years in captivity, when the apartheid government would not allow his image to be seen or his words quoted, most of the world's media did not go out of their way to shine a light on the struggle he led—not until the day of his release from prison, when they competed feverishly to find exclusive angles that were still often superficial. Even then, many of them substituted superficial coverage for analytical reporting, treating him as a celebrity and not the leader of a people's movement.

Many people throughout South Africa and around the world have a point of view as to what Madiba's story should or should not be. But ultimately I am the custodian of the rights to *Long Walk to Freedom*—he entrusted me with turning his story into a motion picture. At the end of the day, I have done my best, and I believe the film is a fitting tribute—to Madiba, to our people's struggle, to Madiba's legacy.

I DIDN'T FEEL my responsibility ends with the movie, so I also produced a three-hour-long in-depth documentary series for television featuring original interviews and insights, archival footage, and short clips from the movie, to ferret out many of the facts (and feelings) we didn't know, and to look at the meaning of the story as well as the making of the movie.

Danny Schechter, an American who has covered Mandela and the struggle closely, and whose involvement with South Africa goes back to the 1960s, directed this effort to bring the story into the present with input from the cast in the movie and "the cast" of the real story—Mandela's lifelong friends and associates. I also invited him to compile this book based on his interviews and reportage. In doing so, Danny has gone well beyond the task he was given. In *Madiba A to Z: The Many Faces of Nelson Mandela*, Danny Schechter has written a unique book, one that wrestles with the true inner complexity and historical drama of the man and his story, blending together other people's insights and his own.

I CAN'T THANK everyone who helped us finish *Long Walk to Freedom*. The list is too long, and their efforts too great to do justice to their contributions. May the movie itself stand as the best thanks. Your efforts have inspired ours.

I must acknowledge again, with deep gratitude, Madiba's trust in my vision, together with my family's support for my long walk that, like his, goes on.

—Anant Singh
Durban, South Africa

Anant Singh is the producer *of Mandela: Long Walk to Freedom*, among many other films made in South Africa. He originally commissioned *Madiba A–Z: The Many Faces of Nelson Mandela* by Danny Schechter.

SEARCHING FOR THE MEANING

Danny Schechter

THIS STORY has been told before, but many never tire of hearing it again: a young African boy, born in South Africa's Eastern Cape, a rural land known for its rolling hills, deep veld, natural beauty, and tribal values, set out on a trajectory that led to his emergence as a world-famous revolutionary who helped build a movement that transformed his country and left a lasting imprint on the world.

Among those who have told that story is Nelson Mandela himself, who, in an autobiography first illegally written by hand in prison, defined his life story as a "long walk to freedom," painting his own picture of the obstacles he overcame and the challenges he faced in a life and death battle against oppression and apartheid.

The book he wrote with that title is now a classic in the literature by and about great freedom fighters. It was published in many languages before being turned into a major motion picture in 2013, based on his diligently told tale and on its interpretation by screenwriter William Nicholson, who faced the daunting task of turning a more than 600-page book into a coherent and dramatic script that brings that story to the screen.

MAKING THE film of Mandela's story—in all of its panoramic sweep and glory and yet with its fine sensibility too—is far more challenging than it already would be because so many people think they already know it.

For the people of South Africa, Mandela was the leader with whom they could identify. He was one of them, had suffered alongside them. They could relate to his story in personal terms. But they also recognized just how much they needed him. They needed a Mandela to bring them together, to help them find a future together, to create a positive future that, without him, was anything but clear.

He understood that, too—and played the role even when it was in conflict with his more political instincts to promote the collective rather than his own personal position. To believe in themselves, many South Africans needed to believe in him, someone who validated their suffering, and who had support and recognition from the world beyond the boundaries of South Africa.

He was always careful in what he said and how he said it, and was often a note taker. That was part of his legal training, a methodology he never abandoned. He often redacted, censored himself so as to protect others, as when he told his biographer Anthony Sampson to omit certain comments he had made that might upset the person he was commenting on. Tim Couzens, one of the writers who helped on his last book, *Conversations with Myself*, also noted how meticulous Mandela had been in his approach. And several researchers on that project have praised him for always reassuring family members how much he cared about them. He may have been cut off from them in prison, but he was very conscious of his duty to praise his children and his wife and to try to motivate them from afar. His letters were his way of carving out a presence for himself in their lives. For someone whose main focus was always the struggle of his people for their freedom, his style had a natural warmth to it, and his life was a deeply personal one.

SAHM VENTER, a journalist turned researcher who has transcribed and read the transcripts of over seventy hours of taped conversations with Mandela, said, "I could shut out the world and listen to the tone, timbre, and speech patterns and the incredibly simple and wise way in which Madiba communicates—a man who went through hell and came out the other side with his soul, beliefs, and dignity intact."

Mac Maharaj spent twelve years on Robben Island with Mandela. And it was Maharaj who then smuggled the manuscript of *Long Walk to Freedom* to London; we have him to thank for the manuscript that survived. He shared, "I must say that Madiba is a very difficult person to get to know at an intimate level. He has a technique of being very warm with anybody and everybody. In fact, he has a unique characteristic that when he shakes hands with a stranger and then meets that person twenty years later, you feel he is giving you his total attention. Nothing else exists and you come out of it extremely pleased with yourself. Your self-esteem goes up and you feel he has given you special recognition. So there's a huge intimacy when he meets you but at the same time when you start interacting with him, there's a shutter. You can't get close to his personal life."

In a letter Mandela wrote to Winnie in 1976, he admitted to

this shutter: "I have been fairly successful in putting on a mask behind which I have pined for the family alone, never rushing for the post when it comes until somebody calls out my name," he wrote. "I am struggling to suppress my emotions as I write this letter."

He didn't suppress his love for Winnie and kept her picture prominently displayed in his cell, but at the same time he also displayed a *National Geographic* photo of a bare-breasted woman he called Nolitha. He joked to his colleagues that he kept the other photo on his desk to make Winnie "jealous." Most writing about Mandela doesn't capture his playfulness.

There were those who were puzzled by his many roles and personas as he kept observers guessing about just who he was and what he was thinking, at times quiet and deliberative, at other times very public and commanding. He was a man with an evolving mystique.

Biographer Anthony Sampson, who edited *Drum Magazine* in South Africa, and who knows the country well, noted in his book, *Mandela: The Authorized Biography*, that even after he was released from captivity, "He still seem[ed] to keep his prison cell inside of him, protecting him from the outside world, controlling his emotions, providing a philosopher's detachment."

As his prison-contracted sickness returned in the mid-1990s, Mandela was still masking his emotions, remaining dignified as he silently struggled to hold onto his inner life and health. The South African academic Sarah Nuttall wrote: "With the fact of his late old age comes the sense that he marks a deep void at the heart of a place that has always struggled to mask what it feels might be an emptiness at its center"—a struggle, Nuttall seemed to be saying, that mirror's a people's struggle "to define itself as a nation and to draw together its many fragments into a sustained sense of commonality, in the wake of a long racist past."

I'VE BEEN privileged to direct nine documentary films about Mandela, several on the invitation of Anant Singh, and one at the personal invitation of Madiba. I traveled alongside Mandela in many settings—in South Africa, around southern Africa, in Europe, Canada, and America. But I don't want to exaggerate the closeness of our relationship. Although he often signaled that he was aware of my presence and schmoozed with me, like many others I experienced the limits to our closeness. While I do consider other top African National Congress (ANC) leaders—Thabo Mbeki, Joe Slovo, and others—to be friends, I consider Mandela to be a man whom I admire, whom I have covered, and who has inspired me, not a friend or a buddy.

I did get to observe him closely in public settings, as he swept into a rally or event, as he spoke with the dry calculation of a politician but with little of the self-promoting demagoguery I associate with politicians. He knew how to get crowds to respond to him, to make a splash, and then, to exit with grace. Sometimes, as I watched him campaign for twelve to fourteen hours day after day, I couldn't fathom where his energy came from.

His time was always planned and managed by his support team and the bodyguards who looked after him dutifully. Little was left to chance. You often felt like Mandela was a role he had been assigned, but at other times you saw his sincerity, his sense of humor and his dedication, especially when he cracked that big smile, and couldn't conceal that he enjoyed all the attention.

WHAT I have set out to do in *Madiba A–Z: The Many Faces of Nelson Mandela* isn't to retell the story that so many biographers and Mandela himself have told, but to seek out deeper reflections and nuances—partly from what we call the "backstory" from the actors in the film as well as the actors in real life, his comrades in the ANC and even some of his adversaries; partly from Mandela himself; and partly by assembling my own thoughts and insights into this most amazing of lives lived.

The device I have used in *Madiba A to Z* is to create what are essentially short essays around themes ranging from the most personal—bullying or forgiveness—to the least personal—negotiations in which Mandela consciously foreswore his own personal desires and political beliefs in order to achieve the greater good by sheer force of . . . compromise. Each letter in this A to Z is written as a self-contained narrative drawing on the Mandela literature, original research, reporting, interviews, press reports, and documents. This is not an academic tome, but high-energy snack food meant for readers used to being media snackers. My goal here is to welcome readers to join the conversation at a deep level. The future not only of South Africa, but of world politics generally, lies in the balance. In the pages before you, you will hear Mandela and many others say that the long walk to freedom is far from over. My hope is that before you are done you'll feel you have something to say about that, something to contribute to our shared future.

ARCHBISHOP Desmond Tutu told me recently, reflecting on the years of struggle, "We were an incredible bunch of people who were mostly very, very idealistic and ready to be self-effacing . . .

because, for one thing, no one knew whether they were going to survive until freedom came."

I have many to thank from among the living, who carry the torch, and from among the dead, who'll always be remembered. From my conversations with Nelson Mandela, and with both his former wife Winnie and with his current wife, Graça, I have learned so much. To all the prominent and not so prominent South Africans who agreed to be interviewed, I give my sincere thanks for the fabulous energy you all brought to our interviews. There were more than 150 of you. I was so fortunate to work with Nicci Bothma as my film editor and Jan Du Toit as my cinematographer on the documentary series, as well as Czerina Patel, who booked interviews and our transcribers and drivers, and the many dedicated teams that helped with my films and our amazing Globalvision series, *South Africa Now*, as well as our human rights follow up, *Rights and Wrongs*, anchored by the gutsy Charlayne Hunter-Gault, who later lived in South Africa for years.

It is a tearful remembrance that I have of the many South African freedom fighters I knew personally who are no longer with us: Oliver Tambo, Joe Slovo, Walter Sisulu, and Johnny Makatini.

Thankfully, my friends Ronnie Kasrils, Pallo Jordan, Denis Goldberg, and Ahmed "Kathy" Kathrada are still here to argue the great issues with. Special thanks to Colette and David Niddrie, who made their Jo'burg home available to me on my frequent film forays. And, of course, Madiba himself, who let me tag along as part of his entourage.

Artists like Gwi Gwi Mwrebi, who first left South Africa to perform in the London production of *King Kong*; Barney Simon, a founder of the multiracial Market Theatre, an unstoppable creative force on the cultural front; poets Mazisi Kunene and Dennis Brutus; musicians Hugh Masakela and Johnny Clegg; journalists Anton Harber, Peter Magubane, and Allister Sparks. So many more that I cannot mention here. Forgive me for not mentioning you all, for if I did, there would be no room for the book that follows.

I would be remiss not to celebrate my mother and father: Ruth, the poet of nine published collections, and Jerry, the worker who inculcated respect for our shared labor history; my brother Bill, educator, and sister-in-law Sandy, the union organizer; my partners and running mates; and my American comrades in so many struggles and movements for social justice, civil rights, and equality, who nurtured my passions and deepened my commitment to change; and to my daughter Sarah Debs Schechter (SDS), now a Hollywood executive, whose love of movies has strengthened my own.

Dan Simon and my extended Seven Stories Press family nurtured my first book, fifteen books ago, *The More You Watch The Less You Know*, and Dan has dedicated himself to launching this one. My producer, Anant Singh, and Videovision invited me from far-away New York to a front-row seat to their country's history. I owe a very special thanks to Sahm Venter and The Nelson Mandela Centre for Memory for reviewing the manuscript under extreme time constraints.

As Anant and Dan both know, I am a media-maker and a media critic, so I was impressed to find that Mandela was so aware of the dangers of corporate journalism, writing, "Although I read a variety of newspapers from around the country, newspapers are only a poor shadow of reality; their information is important to a freedom fighter not because it reveals the truth, but because it discloses the biases and perceptions of both those who produce the paper and those who read it."

One more I will name: a writer, analyst, and close friend who knew Mandela well "back in the day," and who influenced me so much in our days together at the London School of Economics. Although we were both graduate students, she was my mentor on South Africa, and what a teacher she was. I miss her every day in my heart of hearts: South Africa's brave and always outspoken warrior-mother-writer-journalist-editor-revolutionary-educator, Ruth First.

Man, is her voice ever needed today!

To all who were crushed by apartheid, who died, or were wounded or imprisoned, who were displaced, and discouraged, who suffered deprivations and family breakups, forced exile and relocation, were denied the education or the jobs so that they could not have the future they deserved, were kept impoverished by a system that was there to oppress them in countless ways, in the name of a racist theory that caused so much pain to so many for so long:

We honor and remember you all, to those who survived and still struggle to sustain their faith in the future—and those who died in the service of what's best in humanity.

All praises due to Madiba and comrades, and all who fought back and finally tasted of the fruit, however bitter in some cases, and unfulfilled in others, of his and their labors. And, yes, it is worth repeating: the long walk isn't over. Amandla.

—Danny Schechter
New York City and Durban, South Africa
July and August 2013

Nelson Mandela stands, I suppose, as a mirror to this country, you know? He stands as the mirror of change itself.

—Fana Mokoena, actor, plays Govan Mbeki in
Mandela: Long Walk to Freedom

I detest racialism because I regard it as a barbaric thing, whether it comes from a black man or white man.

—Nelson Mandela, from his first speech from the dock during his trial in 1962

MADIBA
A TO Z

ATHLETE

In prison he spent most of his time inside a cell the size of a double bed, but he ran in place and did push-ups and stomach crunches with fanatical persistence. During a three-year spell in which he shared a larger cell with three other political prisoners, he would infuriate his comrades by waking them up at five every morning with his one-hour runs around the cell's tight periphery.

—*SPORTS ILLUSTRATED*

AS A CHILD, Mandela said, his athletic performance was medio-cre, but he paced his life like an athlete.

One of his greatest triumphs as president was the role he played in supporting the country's rugby team, the Springboks, at a world competition in Johannesburg in 1995. The "Boks" had long been a symbol of white South Africa, and Mandela's backing in turn was a symbolic act that promoted reconciliation and national pride.* Many were surprised and excited after the Boks won that cup championship, and they credited Madiba's support.

Rugby seemed an unlikely instrument to make the country whole. Whites loved the sport; it was, as Mandela told me, their

---

* The event was later memorialized in Clint Eastwood's movie *Invictus*, with Morgan Freeman playing Mandela, and Matt Damon as Francois Pienaar, the team captain.

"religion," and members of the national team, the Springboks, were the white nation's high priests. But black South Africans hated the all-white national team and saw their green jerseys as a loathsome symbol of apartheid oppression.

Sports Illustrated reported:

> What really made him nervous was a game between South Africa and New Zealand at Johannesburg's Ellis Park Stadium. "Honestly, I have never been so tense," the world's grandest grand old man recently confided to me. "I felt like fainting." Mandela is one of the coolest people under fire you could ever hope to meet, but what made these statements all the more remarkable was that the sport in question, rugby, was one for which he had no particular passion and whose rules he did not fully understand. . . .
>
> Mandela may not have understood rugby very well, but he understood the political impact sports could have. That's why he seized on the Rugby World Cup. Mandela— in a tremendous act of self-interested generosity toward the vanquished whites—allowed South Africa to host the tournament, which had been awarded to the country in 1992. And then he convinced his black compatriots to make the Springbok team their own, even though there was only one nonwhite player on the 15-man roster.

His infatuation with athletics was hardly limited to rugby. "Sport has the power to change the world," Mandela has said. "It has the power to inspire. It has the power to unite people in a way that little else does. It speaks to youth in a language they understand."

WHEN YOU delve into Mandela's past, you begin to see what sports really meant to him. Richard Stengel, the *Time* magazine editor who "ghosted" Madiba's memoirs, reminded us that he was not into team sports, preferring to compete as a loner. It was at school that he took up long-distance running and boxing, Mandela told him.

Later, in Johannesburg, he was drawn most to boxing, partly for the discipline of it. *Drum*, the lifestyle pictorial magazine of South Africa, ran a photo essay of him sparring on the roof of a building in Johannesburg with a fighter named Jerry Moloi. That scene is recreated in *Mandela: Long Walk to Freedom*. When the filmmakers found the original building, it was dilapidated and had no elevator. But the scene was important and had to be shot there, so the actors and crew carried hundreds of pounds of camera equipment to the rooftop to shoot the scene.

Even after the South African government forbade all pictures of Mandela, one of him posing as a boxer was widely circulated and became a prized possession for many black South Africans, who posted it on the walls of their shacks. When the government distributed 70,000 copies of a booklet denouncing the African National Congress (ANC), people cut out Mandela's photo, pinned it on walls, and turned the quotes attacking the ANC into quotes supporting it, noted biographer Anthony Sampson.

Before he was arrested, Mandela kept in shape as a boxer by maintaining a ninety-minute daily training routine, including regularly running the length of Commissioner Street, one of

Johannesburg's longest. He worked with weights as well. Sampson wrote in his biography: "Mandela saw boxing in political
terms as a contest which was essentially egalitarian and col-
or-blind, where Africans could triumph over discrimination."
Later, in prison, he kept up his taxing fitness regimen, and,
according to former guard Christo Brand, pestered all of his fellow prisoners to exercise regularly.

In *Long Walk to Freedom*, Mandela wrote:

> I did not enjoy the violence of boxing so much as the sci-
> ence of it. I was intrigued by how one moved one's body
> to protect oneself, how one used a strategy both to attack
> and retreat, how one paced oneself over a match. Boxing
> is egalitarian. In the ring, rank, age, color, and wealth are
> irrelevant. . . . I never did any real fighting after I entered
> politics. My main interest was in training; I found the
> rigorous exercise to be an excellent outlet for tension
> and stress. After a strenuous workout, I felt both men-
> tally and physically lighter. It was a way of losing myself
> in something that was not the struggle. After an eve-
> ning's workout I would wake up the next morning feeling
> strong and refreshed, ready to take up the fight again.

Lest we come away thinking Mandela was not competitive, his
lawyer George Bizos told me this story of a visit to Robben Island
when guards gave him and his client tea and something to eat.
Recalled Bizos, "So they brought a wonderful tray of sandwiches
and I noticed that I was having more sandwiches than Nelson
was having. And I said, 'Why aren't you having more?' He then

said that someone—I don't remember who—had beaten him at tennis a couple of days earlier, and he had decided to become fitter in order to take his revenge. Now that was quite an eye-opener for me, as to the special place that sports had for him."

After Mandela began to travel outside of South Africa and tour the world, professional boxers sought him out in droves. That was especially true in June 1990, at a celebrity event organized by Filmmakers and Artists against Apartheid at Robert De Niro's Restaurant, Tribeca Grill, in Lower Manhattan. Police sharpshooters were on the ready outside the event, but inside Mandela had a phalanx of fighters looking after him.

Not everyone in his entourage was taken with his boxing fanaticism. Former ANC leader Cheryl Carolus told this story about a fight they had a few years later about the fight game:

"We were in Edinburgh. We were having breakfast, and everything was fairly easy before the serious stuff, where we have to go into this room with the heads of state from the EU, where they all want a piece of him. So now we're just doing some fairly light banter over breakfast.

"And then he starts talking about boxing. And I say to him, 'Don't be ridiculous, boxing is barbaric.'

"Well, I tell you, he goes onto a serious tirade. And I was saying, 'No, I can't understand why you would put yourself up to be hit by another human being. Secondly, how could you just beat someone to a pulp until they're unconscious? I just think this is barbaric.'

"Well, all I can say is that it turned into a complete knock-down, drag-out fight. A real spat between the two of us. And after it we agreed on two things: first, that we should never ever again speak about boxers and boxing, and secondly, certainly not on an empty stomach.

"It was disastrous! Once we had a function at the [South African] High Commission [in London], and there was the fighter Lenox Lewis, who had sort of bribed his way in. He wasn't on the guest list, but he heard Nelson Mandela was there, and he said, 'I have to meet this man.' So in he comes, and he's this really tall guy, quite a distinctive-looking face. To me he was lost in the huge crowd. But then Madiba arrives, and out of this sea of people he sees Lenox Lewis—and slips away from all the VIPs and the ministers who were there to go to him. 'I've always wanted to meet you,' Mandela tells Lewis and he goes right into a particular point about a fight Lewis had.

"I was finished, you know. What with all these VIP people waiting to receive him as the head of state. But, yeah, if you want to get his attention, children, babies, and boxing—those are the ways."

BULLY: "WILD BRANCHES"

NELSON MANDELA'S outer calm, presence, and sense of dignity, qualities that impress so many, are in good measure a product of his upbringing. Growing up in a culture of traditions, where tribal leaders searched for consensus on key issues, he was considered shy and deferential to his elders. Many noted the young Mandela's serious disposition, and some thought he looked like an old man, even as a teenager.

And yet this peacemaker was pugnacious in his youth, a rebel long before he was a revolutionary, given to bullying those he disagreed with. He was accused of stealing food from a neighbor's garden, rejected an arranged marriage, and was thrown out of University of Fort Hare for defying the rules.

The South African actor Atandwa Kani, who studied Mandela's childhood closely in preparing to play the part of young Mandela in the movie, saw that just as Mandela was shaped by a traditional society, he also rebelled against it.

"I think he was thinking what any normal kid would be thinking at that age," Kani told me. "You know that the teenage worries are always sort of superficial, but they weigh heavily on you anyway because it's all relative. I think that there was a lot put on him—not on him as an individual, but at that age there was a lot placed upon him because of his lineage, because of his heritage, and the people that he grew up under."

Speaking as a young South African of a more cosmopolitan generation, Kani said, it's hard to understand those emotions. "It's quite difficult to tap into that because on one side he was just a little kid at that point, but . . . he was expected to be much more. You know, the leader of his nation. . . ."

I pushed him a bit, saying, "In a way this is an unlikely story, because here he is growing up in a very poor tribal-denominated area, tied to a royal family. The thought of him becoming the leader of a nation, or a hero of the world, would have been so far off from his thinking, or anyone's thinking."

Kani replied almost cosmically, "This is what you could call a situation that was written in the stars. He was destined for greatness regardless—whether he had stayed in the village and become the chief and looked after his people and become that great man, or, like he did: move to Jo'burg, studied at a law firm, and become this great man now. I suppose whatever situation Mandela was put in, he would have risen to the occasion and become a great man. It was inevitable."

"Was his first revolutionary act rejecting an arranged marriage?" I asked.

Kani thought for a minute, then commented, "When we talk about the traditions that we go through, it's almost set in stone what you will do, according to your elders. They have your life set out for you, especially at that time, where it was you were obligated to do these things. Nowadays we have more of a voice. But back then it was more stringent and more strict. And for someone that age to reject that which was a cultural practice, it's almost unheard of. He was really, really brave."

A white comrade of Mandela's, Denis Goldberg, who was also

sent to prison for taking part in the armed struggle, agreed with me that rejecting tradition is what first turned Mandela into a revolutionary:

"My understanding of Nelson Mandela is that he becomes a revolutionary when he refuses to marry the girl selected for him, as the son of a minor chief. He rejects tradition. Steals some cows to get the fare money to go to Johannesburg to see what's over the hill. He's never to my knowledge used his chiefly inheritance to justify his leadership. He's a leader because of his intellect and his ability to analyze and to inspire others. He has been able to do what I think a leader has to do, and that is to draw people together to follow an agreed course of action."

MANDELA WAS often impetuous, and quickly became part of the ANC Youth League that challenged the veteran leaders, and even many in the Communist Party, because he was more taken with African Nationalism.

ANC strategist Joel Netshitenzhe described how some of the old-line leaders believed Mandela had what they called "wild branches": "Sisulu, Dadoo, and others saw some qualities of leadership in Madiba. But they also saw that there were wild branches in his body. They helped to prune them. He himself talks about how he used to break up meetings of people he couldn't agree with, how sometimes when he relates to people he shows a level of pride that might not help in the building of that bridge of relationship. So those leaders saw the good qualities in him, but they accepted that he had weaknesses, and helped him to correct the weakness and build the good qualities."

Kgalema Motlanthe—one-time political prisoner on Robben

Island, labor leader, and then South Africa's deputy president— shared with me what he knows of these wild branches:

"[I]n his young days he used to go and bust up meetings of the Communist Party. One time, there was an old stalwart, J. B. Marks, who was the leader of the ANC as well as the leader of the Communist Party, and so he says he went and disrupted this meeting, spoke about 'Red bull' and 'Black bull,' and Madiba says, you know, his arguments were completely incoherent.

"But he says one other thing: that these old leaders of the Communist Party never ever attacked him or criticized him in public. Instead, the general secretary of the party at that time, Moses Kotane, sought an appointment with Madiba. And Madiba says, well, you know, he wasn't confirming any appointment—until one day when he got home from work [and] found Moses Kotane waiting for him at his house.

"Moses Kotane said, 'Well, I've been trying to secure an appointment with you with no luck, so I'm here. I think you should know that I've already discussed with your wife that I'm sleeping here tonight so that we can discuss things.' And he says Moses Kotane asked him why he hates Communists so much, and have Communists ever oppressed him, because all we want is to be involved in the same struggle? And so he says they discussed it, and by the time they retired he was convinced that Communists are our allies."

At the time, the Communist Party stood alone as the only ethnically mixed political organization in South Africa, where whites, blacks, Indians, and coloreds (i.e., neither black nor white) were equally welcome, thus was popular as a refuge for those who didn't want to define their politics in nationalistic, racial, or ethnic terms.

I find Motlanthe's story ironic, because the apartheid system labeled Mandela a Communist, even when he insisted he wasn't. More recently, a new book by Stephen Ellis "revealed" that he once was—but that claim has not been widely accepted.

In one of his earlier trials, Mandela had been put on a list of Communists. His lawyer, at his direction, sued, saying the allegation was false, and the government later took him off the list. The "proof" of his party membership revolved around his attendance at a meeting in 1960. Witnesses told the author that only Communists would have been there. That, however, is based on speculation—not proof.

Motlanthe jumped in, "Of course. Of course, yes. Once they passed the Suppression of Communism Act, they used the Act to restrict people's movements, to banish them, to place them under house arrest. It was used as justification for all manners of restrictions.

"Well, he never really asked of others what he himself would not be prepared to do," said the deputy president. "So when it came to pass that, you know, the program of action, which was inspired by the Youth League of his generation, was to be implemented in the defiance of unjust law campaign, he was the 'volunteer in chief,' and again when the decision was made to resort to armed struggle, and for the ANC to continue as an illegal organization, he was again at the forefront. . . . He led from the front, and that inspires confidence in ordinary members of the ANC."

I asked Motlanthe, "Could his comrades criticize him? Was he open to debate and discussion, or was he headstrong?"

"He is open while he's shaping his position. But once he has taken a position, he's very resolute," was Motlanthe's response.

"Resolute?"

"Very resolute, very resolute."

ARCHBISHOP Desmond Tutu spoke to me of his belief that South Africa is lucky that Mandela returned to political life when he did because he was less angry and much more thoughtful. Tutu credited his years behind bars.

"Prison mellowed him wonderfully," he suggested. "As you know, he went to prison a very angry, youngish man. I mean, the commander in chief of the military wing of the ANC . . . so he was pretty aggressive."

Tutu laughed out loud when I told him that some of his comrades spoke of Madiba's wild branches that had to be pruned.

Tutu turned reflective. "It's amazing. Frequently people say, 'Just look at that, he's done twenty-seven years. What a waste!' But had he come out earlier . . . we would have had the angry, aggressive Madiba. As a result of the experience that he had there, he mellowed. . . . Suffering either embitters you or, mercifully, ennobles you. And with Madiba, thankfully for us, the latter happened. He grew in his magnanimity. He became able to put himself in the shoes of the other. . . . When he came out, only someone like him could have said to—especially these young angry types—that no, we've got to go for negotiations. Very many of them had expected that they were going to march into Pretoria at the ends of the barrels of their guns. And only someone with the credibility that he had developed, you know, because no one could say to him, 'You're saying all of these things because you know nothing about suffering.' Well, twenty-seven years. . . . It's just incontrovertible."

COMRADE

MANY OF the dictionaries in the Western world still speak of the term "comrade" as if it is associated only with communist parties, but its use embraces labor and social movements as well. During the French Revolution, titles of nobility were abolished, and *monsieur* and *madame* (literally, "my lord" and "my lady") were replaced by *citoyen* for men and *citoyenne* for women (both meaning "citizen"). The deposed King Louis XVI, for instance, was referred to as *Citoyen Louis Capet* to emphasize his loss of privilege. When the socialist movement gained momentum in the mid-nineteenth century, socialists began to look for an egalitarian alternative to terms like "mister," "miss," or "missus." Ultimately they chose "comrade" as their preferred term of address.

Nelson Mandela's African National Congress, and its allies in the labor unions and Communist Party, all used the term "comrade" to project a common identity and show mutual respect. Beyond the salutation, there's another meaning of great value to Mandela: the idea of a community based on comradeship.

Many of the former prisoners I met on Robben Island, at a reunion of ex-prisoners in 1995, said that the *comradeship* they shared with each other allowed them to cope with the brutal prison experience.

The Rivonia Trial defendants who were sent to "the Island"

worked closely together as a team. Two were acquitted, the rest given life sentences, including the two white defendants.

They respected each other and they relied on each other, consulting on political issues and finding ways to be supportive, even though they heard each other's stories endlessly, sometimes to the point of boredom.

They saw Mandela as their leader, although there was also a formal decision-making body called "the high organ" run by the Communists in the group who believed in a Marxist-style centralized hierarchy. Mandela was seen as "leading from the back," as he explained in his *Long Walk to Freedom*: "A leader . . . is like a shepherd. He stays behind the flock, letting the most nimble go out ahead, whereupon the others follow, not realizing that all along they are being directed from behind."

Former prisoner Laloo Chiba confirmed that "the comrades" often had differences with each other, and sometimes that led to tension, even violence. He credited Mandela, Sisulu, and Kathrada with restoring calm: "There were a lot of debates that we had, you know. You live in prison conditions, tensions are high, the pressure from the warders, and of course you are also frustrated, and under those conditions people do tend to boil over sometimes, not physically but in other ways . . . but Kathy [Ahmed Kathrada] was always calm, ensuring that he brought order and stability into any relationship."

I interjected: "Even when fights threatened, even when people were ready to go at each other?"

"Yes. He was still calm. One of the things about Kathy, like Madiba, like Walter, when there were problems, they always moved to the front row to absorb the shocks and the pressures.

A pensive Nelson Mandela, in 1951, with journalist Ruth First. JURGEN SCHADEBERG

But when things were calm, when things were okay, when things were running smoothly, like Walter, like Madiba, they moved right to the back. That's one of the great things about any leader."

THE PRISONERS were up against rules and routines designed to break their spirit, but, in retrospect, many now say they had it easier than their comrades on the outside. Ahmed Kathrada, who became very close to Mandela, spoke to the sense that they were, in some ways, lucky: "What sustained us also on Robben Island, besides the longest expectation, was the knowledge, all the time we were suffering in prison, although it was not a picnic, although it was hard, that as difficult as it was, there was always the knowledge that while we were having it difficult inside, our comrades outside were in the cold face of the struggle. In a sense we were protected, because no policeman could come to Robben Island and start shooting at us. We were protected. Our comrades outside were not.

"Many of them were tortured, many were killed. We were protected. The 600 who were killed in the Soweto Uprising, they were in the cold face of the struggle. We were not. I think that sometimes the suffering of the prisoners is exaggerated, in a sense. I must emphasize that I am not trying to minimize the hardship of prison, but on Robben Island, and for political prisoners as a whole, we were not the core of the struggle. That was taking place outside Robben Island, in the country, in exile. That was the core of the struggle."

That may be, but at the time the prisoners were being challenged every day by hostile warders, repressive conditions, and arbitrary orders. Former prison guard Christo Brand told me that he and his colleagues were required to be brutal. Brand is a native Afrikaans-speaker; English was, as for many white South Africans, particularly those with little education, his second or even third language. He revealed the harsh calculation in the prison's methodology in his rapid-fire Afrikaner-inflected English: "Prisoners must do hard labor. We must keep them physically and mentally hard-working, breaking stones, making this, doing that in the limestone quarry, whatever will make them so tired in the evening when they get back to their cells they can't think to make something, uprising, whatever. They are too tired. The must just eat, relax and fall asleep.

"The next day: push them again. And through this hard labor we keep them, in a way, fit. And the food is also bad. And that was prison's way to break the person down, to rehabilitate him in prison with hard labor. That's why we were brutal on them. You will see there was a few incidents that happened where they dig a hole and urinate on one of the prisoners, that type of thing happened. Brutality happened."

Resisting brutality gave the prisoners a common struggle and brought them together. Writing in *Foreign Affairs*, Africa scholar Fran Buntman concluded that it was the conditions in prison that fostered the will to find effective forms of resistance: "A common spirit of resistance helped them develop habits of mutual tolerance and construct autonomous social and political structures outside the authority of their warders. Assimilation of new inmates and the release of old ones helped to spread organizational tactics and knowledge back into the wider political struggle; experience acquired through interactions with prison authorities prepared a cadre of leaders with the patience and bargaining skills necessary to negotiate an eventual settlement with the regime."

Raymond Suttner of the ANC found Buntman's research of value: "A key element of the book is understanding the responses of the prisoners as an attempt to create an alternative world insofar as they come to control more and more of their lives, albeit within a situation of incarceration. They were able to establish a culture that was in the first place a continuation of the political cultures of their respective organizations prior to imprisonment, although the African National Congress (ANC) was able, partly through its numbers and partly through its long experience, to achieve this process most effectively."

White prisoners like Denis Goldberg have said they had it harder than the blacks because they had less support and were considered traitors. He told us, "The attitude was—and I experienced this throughout the twenty-two years from my arrest to my release, from the lowest policeman and prison guard, to generals—'We don't like Nelson Mandela, but we respect him for fighting for his people. But you, Goldberg, we hate you. 'Cause you have betrayed us, because you are white.' And the hatred was palpable throughout."

The filmmakers and production designers worked imaginatively not only to depict this harsh reality but also to create an environment to show the comradeship of the prisoners in action.

The actor Fana Mokoena (Govan Mbeki) said, "I think it's an amazing environment for a performer. [Movie director Justin Chadwick] has kind of made it too easy, but very difficult as well—because it's almost too real. But that's what he wanted to create from the onset. . . . He doesn't want to see Mandela the hero, he wants to see the man. He wants to see how these men were tired every day. He wants to see them scared, almost half crying. He wants to see them cold, he wants to see them happy. He wants to see the people. And he's created that environment for that to happen, which has been really quite amazing."

In a 1996 interview with archivist Padraig O'Malley, Ahmed Kathrada stressed the positive aspects of comradeship that sustained the men's morale:

What one misses very much is the camaraderie, the very close contact with friends and colleagues, although we were of course confined to one section of the prison, the B section where the president and, on average, about twenty or twenty-five of us stayed. But we also had the advantage in our section of prison, the fortunate advantage of being in the presence of outstanding individuals, political leaders, academicians, and just your average person of exceptional quality. . . .

Over the years that we shared together, we built a very unique sort of relationship with one another. . . . You know, you build a relationship where you are free with each other, you are frank with one another, you criticize one another, you accept criticism, you make observations, you analyze situations. It was very easy and informal.

Out in the world here you are thrust into bureaucracy, into a lot of formality where you are not able to have these extensive relaxed discussions as you had in prison. Those are the things one misses and much of it brings back fond memories both of a serious nature and more light-hearted. One misses also the atmosphere free, or relatively free, of tensions because as the years went by there was relaxation, there was less and less harassment so that we were free of tension, we had time to think, we had time to discuss seriously, we had time for fun. One misses all that.

What they didn't miss were rules that led to deep feelings of isolation: strict silence in their cells, twenty-three-hour lockups on weekends and public holidays with little time for exercise. They were ordered to sleep at 8:00 p.m., but lights were kept on. Working in the very white lime quarry left them covered in dust. In Mandela's case, the dust damaged his tear ducts. To the government, his cell was meant to be his tomb.

Mandela responded by finding something to do that took him outside the austere cells, in his case, tending a garden. The Nigerian poet Wole Soyinka once wrote, "Your Logic Frightens Me, Mandela," in which he compares Mandela's patience to that of a gardener. Unknown to Soyinka, that's what Mandela became.

Elleke Boehmer wrote, "Given how many prison hours were spent in introspective seclusion, gardening became especially important to Mandela, as it has to other political prisoners, as a link to the material world."

In 1975, working with Laloo Chiba—a former commander in the ANC's armed wing Umkhonto we Sizwe (MK), the Spear of the Nation—they raised two thousand chilies, one thousand tomatoes, and two watermelons, as well as peppers and cucumbers. The gardening continued when Prisoner 466/64 became 220/82 at Pollsmoor Maximum Security Prison. Some of the fresh vegetables from Mandela's gardens were given to the guards, others were used for special meals on Sundays.

Boehmer continued, "How to explain the sustained importance of gardening to the prisoner Mandela? For one, from the perspective of a self-styled 'country boy,' the pleasures of working the earth no doubt recalled the rural environment of his childhood . . . for another, in his garden he could practice prudence, self-sufficiency, and provident planning."

Mandela himself has said, "In prison, a garden is one of the few things you can really master and call your own. . . . The feeling of being the steward of this tiny patch of earth is a small taste of freedom."

There was also a spirit of compassionate concern in what were called the "single cells," even for prisoners who came from other political parties, like Eddie Daniels.

Daniels was the only member of the Liberal Party behind bars, serving a fifteen-year sentence for sabotage. He told me one story that captured why he came to love Madiba and the community he led. It also speaks to the way Mandela and "the comrades" looked after each other:

"I was sick in jail. We were not allowed to go to the hospital. . . . I'm laying on the floor. Madiba comes back from the quarry and he says to someone, 'Where is Danny?'

"They say, 'Danny is lying on the floor in his cell, he is sick.' Madiba's cell is at the bottom of the corridor, my cell is right at the top. He walks all the way up to my cell, sits on the floor and comforts me. Then he's locked up in his cell, I'm locked up in mine.

"The next morning . . . our cells are opened up for us to go and clean our buckets because we haven't got running water or flush toilets. So we go into the common toilet and clean our buckets.

"So Madiba walks all the way up the corridor to my cell with his bucket on his arm. Puts his bucket on the floor, sits down next to me, and he comforts me. He comforts me. Then he stands up puts his bucket over his arm, puts my bucket over his other arm, and he goes to the common toilet, cleans my bucket, brings it back to me.

"Now, to put the story into context, Madiba, an international figure, the most important leader of the most powerful organization fighting the apartheid government, the most important prisoner in South Africa, he could have instructed any of his members to look after Danny. He came to look after me himself, freely, not because he had to."

Even as he supported the collective and often spoke in its name, he also asserted his own personality and style as a leader who stood out from the others, yet kept the respect of the group.

Historian Verne Harris of the Nelson Mandela Centre of Memory saw a conflict within him. "It's a tension that has played out inside of him too because there's a part of him that enjoys the adulation, there's a vanity. He enjoys the crowds and the elevation. But there's another part that precisely feels uncomfortable with that. 'I'm part of a collective, I've always relied on others. I've had mentors, I'm part of a movement.' . . . It's complex."

Sahm Venter works alongside Verne at the Centre. She calls herself a "recovering" journalist, and is absorbed in a deeper analysis of Madiba's role. She has become critical of the way her former colleagues treat personalities like Mandela.

She told me, "Well isn't that what the media does? The media likes to pick out a character. I mean, here's a perfect person that Walter Sisulu found to front the organization, but having said that, Madiba often strays away from the collective. For example, when he was in Pollsmoor Prison and he started talking to the government, he didn't purposefully tell his comrades until it was kind of too late because he was such a democrat, because he knew that if all of those people had said 'don't do it' he would've stopped and we would not have reached democracy when we did."

He anticipated criticism and sometimes even asked for it.

Venter, who is now more of a historian than a reporter, explained, "At that time, when they were in the trenches with the National Party, it was difficult. But from what I understand, when he became president, and in the run up, he would enjoy being criticized and say, 'Well, just give me your best shot and I'll argue my way out of it.' I suppose you know he's a human being, having gone through everything he did, and then to get some question he regards as impudent or whatever. He's human."

Sometimes he seemed superhuman, perhaps because of his discipline.

On April 10, 1993, Mandela was interrupted for a phone call in the middle of a formal reception. Over the phone, he was told that ANC leader Chris Hani had just been killed. Mandela was shaken, and put the phone down to reflect on the ominous news. After a minute of silence, he returned to the reception line without telling anyone what he had just learned.

He became tougher as he moved into the next phase, outside of prison. "He could be dismissive," said Venter, who recalled the way he stood up to then South African President de Klerk's attack on the ANC during the multiparty Convention for a Democratic South Africa (CODESA) talks, which took place in 1991 and 1992.

"That was amazing. I mean that was classic Madiba. No prepared speech. He just got back up on that stage and he let him have it, you know, cutting him off at the knees. He could do that. I think he stands with a great deal of moral authority."

If, at times, he lost his cool, slamming the table and wagging his finger at underlings—if as Verne Harris said, he was "not a saint"—it was because he knew how important it was to express his views. So although Mandela, most of the time, was the best of comrades, he also believed that sometimes this meant going in the opposite direction. As Mandela himself would say, "Good leaders lead."

DIPLOMAT

LONG BEFORE he advocated, on his own, for the release of his prison comrades and himself, and long before he led the ANC delegation into talks with the all-white apartheid government, Mandela already had, as a trial lawyer, a lot experience in the diplomatic area. Though while a prisoner he insisted that he was "facilitating," to make clear that he wasn't in a position to negotiate in jail, he was already considered a fiery speaker, even an agitator, prior to his prison days—once almost tossed out of the ANC for calling for action without a plan—and gradually developed into a highly competent negotiator, well tempered in formal talks.

His exposure as a child to tribal decision-making stressed consensus rather than conflict. This may have played its part in key choices Mandela made. The tribal culture in which he grew up was one where reason and fairness informed the outcomes of disputes.

"HE WAS A good listener and he was an analytical thinker," former South African president F. W. de Klerk said of Mandela. "Both of us are lawyers, and therefore the communication was well structured and logical."

De Klerk told me he was also able to feel more relaxed because of Madiba's sense of humor and his way making even his enemies comfortable:

"At that very first meeting which we had, we avoided discussing anything of real substance. We were just feeling each other out. We were sort of discussing the history of the Anglo-Boer War. He was a great admirer of General Devoet and other Afrikaner generals. We had in common our feeling that it was an unjust war initiated by the British Empire. But we did not talk about the issues of the day.

"I could report afterwards to my constituency, 'I think I can do business with this man.' And in his *Long Walk to Freedom*, [Mandela] writes that after that first meeting, he could report back he thought he could do business with me. I think that very first meeting laid a foundation which outlasted lots of onslaughts . . . and which resulted, in our later days, in a good friendship between us."

In his initial discussions with government, he was at a disadvantage. He was one man up against an adversary with a whole bureaucracy behind it. He often prepared for these meetings the way a lawyer would—writing key points to be raised in a notebook, laying out his message points and also verbalizing the questions he was posing. He seemed to be in a constant dialogue with himself. He might write, "Suggestions for Stopping Violence," and then add this note: "Can we remain indifferent to the slaughter and continue to talk to the regime?" In one notebook, he wrote, "A cardinal point that we must keep constantly in mind, the lodestar which keeps us in course, as we negotiate the uncharted twists and turns of the struggle for liberation is that the breakthrough is never the result of individual effort. It is always a collective effort and triumph." He realized that as a political leader, he was always, in the end, representing his own constituency, and this added fire to his oratory.

Mandela knew how to use flattery and praise and then, just as quickly, might become argumentative and even accusatory. He understood that diplomacy demands give and take—being seductive one moment, firm the next, and then, even funny. In their later talks he angrily accused de Klerk of promoting violence and representing an illegitimate government. But then he turned around and, to the anguish of some of his supporters, praised him as a "man of integrity." Mandela played the part of diplomat much like he played Creon in Sophocles' drama *Antigone*, when he was a prisoner on Robben Island.

The *Mail & Guardian* reported in 1999 on that performance:

> One year in the late 1960s, the play chosen for performance at Christmas by inmates of South Africa's notorious Robben Island prison was *Antigone*. In Athol Fugard's memorable version of the event in *The Island*, Sophocles was given a new lease on life, with particular and poignant relevance to the struggle for liberation from apartheid in South Africa. In the Robben Island production, the man who volunteered to play Creon had very little stage experience, his only prior role of some note having been, significantly, that of John Wilkes Booth, president Abraham Lincoln's assassin, in a college show. That man was Nelson Rolihlahla Mandela. Although, like his fellow actors, he primarily identified with Antigone, he brought to the interpretation of Creon what must have been, in retrospect, a peculiar insight: "Of course you cannot know a man completely, his character, his principles, sense of judgment, not till he's

shown his color, ruling the people, making laws. Experience, there's the test.

Mandela was a close student of South Africa's political history
and made a point of learning about Afrikaner history, often in
the Afrikaans language. He pushed himself to understand more
deeply the culture and mindset of his adversaries and oppressors.

His biographer, Anthony Sampson, told an interviewer for
public television in America:

> He learned Afrikaans in prison. This wonderful, precise,
> very scholarly Afrikaans. He would often, when telling
> me a story about prison, say something in Afrikaans, a
> language unfortunately which I don't speak, and then he
> would take my pad and he'd painstakingly write it out
> in his big capital letter print. I was looking at my notes
> before, and this one time when they used the word for
> "stomach," saying to one of the prisoners, "You will lose
> that big stomach when you are in here." They used the
> Afrikaans word for stomach that applies to an animal,
> not a man. And he was very precise in the way he spelled
> it out for me, and explained the distinction between the
> word you use for stomach for a man, and stomach for
> an animal. That was the way he learned Afrikaans. He
> wanted to make sure that he understood the language of
> the enemy. That he could speak it.

Describing the negotiations, Sampson wrote in his book *Mandela: The Authorized Biography*, "It was one of the most spectacular

A classic 1950s street shot of a dapper Mandela—with his distinctive smile and hair-style—alongside Moses Kotane outside the Pretoria Court in 1958, after hearing that the prosecution withheld charges. JURGEN SCHADEBERG

negotiations in history, and Western governments watched it with fascination. While fighting continued in Northern Ireland, Yugoslavia and the Middle East, South Africa was seen as 'the negotiating capital of the world,' and academics, journalists and diplomats converged to observe it."

Responding to a report on the CBS News program *60 Minutes*, a negotiations expert itemized key lessons from his approach:

- Speak the language of the other party.
- Keep your cards very close to the vest.
- Do not doubt your chance at success.
- Be prepared.
- Project confidence.
- Do not be coerced into making unnecessary compromises and/or concessions.

These guidelines all seem simple, but Mandela was in prison at the time he developed them. Some of his comrades were suspicious of individuals reaching out to the government, while others feared Mandela might sell out because he was in such a vulnerable position. It's also important to recall that Mandela was part of a collective leadership, and that other ANC leaders, especially fellow lawyer Joe Slovo, were experienced and skilled negotiators.

Richard Stengel, the *Time* magazine editor who ghosted *Long Walk to Freedom*, wrote about the period when Mandela, now in his own cell at Pollsmoor Prison, away from the men he spent so many years with, decided to talk with the government in 1985:

"Mandela on his own launched the first negotiations with the apartheid government. This was anathema to the African National Congress (ANC). After decades of saying 'prisoners cannot negotiate' and after advocating an armed struggle that would bring the government to its knees, he decided that the time was right to begin to talk to his oppressors."

When he initiated the negotiations, there were many who thought he had lost it. "We thought he was selling out," said Cyril Ramaphosa, then the powerful leader of the National Union of Mineworkers. "I went to see him to tell him, 'What are you doing?' It was an unbelievable initiative. He took a massive risk."

Newspaper editor and writer Allister Sparks, author of *The Mind of South Africa: The Rise and Fall of Apartheid*, was the first to ferret out the details of this secret diplomacy. He told me:

"Mandela himself had twenty-seven meetings with a committee that was headed by the head of the security services in South Africa named Niël Barnard. He had initially met with the minister of prisons and of police. He had met with . . . Kobie Coetsee was his name, via Winnie Mandela. Coetsee had bumped into Winnie Mandela on a plane. Coetsee then encouraged the then–president P. W. Botha to establish this committee.

"Kobie himself first met Mandela when Mandela was having prostate surgery in a hospital in Cape Town, while he was still a prisoner, and that developed into a series of secret meetings that took place. Initially they moved Mandela off of Robben Island to Pollsmoor Prison in Cape Town [in 1982]. Then, later [in 1988], they moved him to a prison in a small- or medium-sized town, the wine land town of Paarl some fifty kilometers outside of Cape Town. That is where the bulk of the secret meetings took place."

These meetings mark Mandela's departure from the role of prisoner and transition to becoming a negotiator, acting as a leader not just with his own comrades, but with the government itself. Sparks commented on the departure: "He had difficulty in communicating all of this to his comrades who were based mainly in Lusaka, but his lawyer here, George Bizos, acted as a kind of intermediary because Bizos could have access, as the lawyer, to Mandela in prison. So he would go and discuss what was happening with Mandela at the prison and then travel to Lusaka."

Mandela had Bizos keep his former law partner—Oliver Tambo, the head of the ANC in Lusaka, Zambia—informed about his conversations. The ANC did not oppose them because Mandela was feeling out the government, not making any deals. He called himself a "facilitator."

Later, Ramaphosa would support him too, as he told *Time*: "'He's a historical man. . . . He was thinking way ahead of us. He has posterity in mind. 'How will they view what we've done?' Prison gave him the ability to take the long view. It had to; there was no other view possible. He was thinking in terms of not days and weeks, but decades. He knew history was on his side, that the result was inevitable; it was just a question of how soon and how it would be achieved. 'Things will be better in the long run,' he sometimes said. He always played for the long run."

The focus of the final talks that followed was on replacing a white-dominated authoritarian system with a multiracial democratic one. The ANC worked to avert a race war and find a way to promote peace and reconciliation. It pushed for the free and fair election that it won, in 1994, with over 60 percent of the vote.

Shaun Johnson, then a newspaper reporter, now the director of the Mandela Rhodes Foundation, was at those final negotiations and observed Mandela's approach:

"I was in the room at the time of the CODESA negotiations

with the National Party government, and heard him say, 'If you don't know what you are prepared to give up, don't negotiate.' And what he meant by that is that he understood that politics is the art of the possible in give and take. So he made compromise acceptable and understandable to people who didn't naturally feel that compromise was necessary."

I told Johnson about arguments being made today suggesting that the settlement was flawed and even that Mandela "sold out." Johnson responded:

"There is a serious debate to be had about what he led in terms of the compromise settlement. I personally believe that without that settlement at that time—it was that time, not now—this country would've descended into the worst racial civil war ever seen on this planet. And we wouldn't be sitting here in these beautiful surrounds. This place would be rubble. And I think that's the answer to it. And I think that for now, people who criticize the ANC and Mr. Mandela for the negotiated settlement, they weren't there.

"The ANC actually negotiated rings around the National Party and got a brilliant settlement at that time without having to fire a shot. And also, I was in the room once long ago when Mr. Mandela said, apropos of a different discussion, 'I did not want to inherit a country without roads.'"

Allister Sparks wasn't especially diplomatic in response to hearing the charge that Mandela sold out.

"The idea that Mandela sold out is absolutely rubbish," he said scornfully. "The main negotiator at that point was actually Joe Slovo, the leader of the Communist Party. He was the one who made some of the critical decisions about the concessions that needed to be reached to arrive at a settlement.

"You have got huge battles taking place today in the ANC, which is split into many fractions. They are fighting each other and, of course, it pays some of them to spread this nonsensical stuff that Mandela sold out.

"Mandela pulled off, as I think the world recognizes, one of the most significant and unique peaceful transitions from authoritarianism to democracy."

TRUE ENOUGH, in *political* terms, but a lack of focus and clarity on economic issues would come back to haunt the ANC when it found itself dominated by the corporate sector and locked into neoliberal compromises that gave it little leverage over the economy. ANC leader, and later government minister, Ronnie Kasrils does not criticize Mandela for avoiding conflicts with the corporate elite in order to assure a peaceful transition to a democratic political order and neutralize the power centers of the apartheid government, but he does concede: "In the early 1990s, we in the leadership of the ANC made a serious error. Our people are still paying the price."

The political battle was won but the economic battle would have to be fought over the long term.

ELOQUENT

IN THE DOCK of the Rivonia Trial in Pretoria's Palace of Justice, Mandela and his comrades were facing charges of sabotage after a police raid on the base for the ANC's armed wing, Umkhonto we Sizwe (MK). After this trial, Mandela would spend the next quarter of a century in prison. But before that sentencing, he made a historic public declaration, against the advice of his lawyers, declaring for all the world to hear that he was prepared to die for his freedom. In essence, Mandela was taunting the state to put him to death.

Mandela's words were not originally televised but they were reported and remembered by millions of South Africans. They are simple, and spoken with intensity and dignity:

"I have fought against white domination, and I have fought against black domination," he proclaims.

"I have cherished the ideal of a democratic and free society in which all persons live together in harmony and with equal opportunities. It is an ideal which I hope to live for and to achieve. But if needs be, it is an ideal for which I am prepared to die."

At first, the defense team had questioned his decision to make such a defiant speech, but he insisted. He had actually delivered a similar oration years before. But, by doing so, under court rules, he prevented the prosecutor from cross-examining him because he acknowledged his "guilt."

He had, from the beginning, insisted on a political defense because the whole spectacle, in his view, was clearly a political trial. Actor Idris Elba, wearing a suit like the one Mandela wore then, on a set that is an exact replica of the original courtroom, does a brilliant reenactment for the movie *Mandela: Long Walk to Freedom*. He recreates that dramatic moment in excruciating detail, and rightly makes it the centerpiece for how the movie presents Mandela's story.

AHMED KATHRADA, one of the defendants, said their lawyer, Bram Fischer, told them, "Chaps, prepare for the worst." All of the defendants were told repeatedly they were going to die, so in a sense, they turned that threat into a preemptive strategy, welcoming their martyrdom.

When his attorney, George Bizos, expressed the concern that Mandela might be giving too much to his political enemies, he agreed to a small revision—to add the words "if needs be" to the statement, so as to make it clear that he was prepared to die, but did not want to die.

Another lawyer, later appointed as South Africa's chief justice, Arthur Chaskalson, said that "right up till he was actually delivering his speech, he was changing it."

The eloquence that Mandela was known for did not flow effortlessly. He considered and organized his words carefully, often writing on long legal pads with no. 2 pencils, a practice that went back to his years in law school where he learned to take detailed notes.

When Mandela later toured the world and began to speak at large rallies and smaller events, audiences flocked to hear him, even when, by that time, many of his speeches were drafted with speechwriters.

Reported the *Los Angeles Times*:

> Many Americans began to identify with the man from South Africa as they have with few world leaders. A New York tabloid called him and his wife, Winnie, the "Apple of Our Eye." Even at the State Department headquarters in Washington, Mandela's arrival to meet with Secretary of State James A. Baker III last week caused a stir.
>
> "Every Foreign Service officer in the building was trying to get down there to see him," said an African analyst there.

The black community was especially thrilled by his reception. Ron Walters, a professor of political science at Washington's black university Howard, added that Mandela's "eloquence, strength, consistency and brilliance" evoked inevitable comparisons with [Martin Luther] King [Jr.], even though Mandela embraces violence as a means of liberating black South Africans, while King was a prophet of nonviolence.

In 1990, Nelson and Winnie Mandela brought flowers to Martin Luther King Jr.'s grave in Atlanta. He said he thought nonviolence was a good policy, when you could be nonviolent. He later quoted King's "I Have a Dream Speech" at a rally in the city that used to call itself "too busy to hate."

Mandela didn't have King's polished Baptist preacher speaking style, but it truly didn't matter, so charmed was the hometown crowd by how deeply Mandela seemed to feel the connection between South Africa's struggle against racial injustice and America's.

Many more were taken by his words than were put off by his often "wooden" way of expressing them.

Few have the courage to go public with even mild criticisms, as former Archbishop Desmond Tutu explained, "When you have right on your side, and you don't have to, you know, think up smart sound bites, you are basically speaking the truth. I think you are on a better wicket than someone who has to keep thinking, 'Oh, am I letting one cat out of the bag or something?'

"One has to say: he is gifted. He's a lousy public speaker, yes. And yet, people are on tenterhooks.

"And I'm not sure that people listen very much to the words he speaks, as to the fact that he communicates who he is. That is eloquent, too."

FORGIVENESS

IF THERE IS one attribute that has endeared Nelson Mandela to millions of supporters, especially in the West, it is for his ability to forgive. Mandela's commitment to reconciliation is a part of a principled policy to forgive the enemies of freedom for the benefit of all in South Africa. Forgive, not forget!

The black leaders who suffered most are agreed on reconciliation, though some less enthusiastically than Mandela. "I couldn't have forgiven my warder two weeks after I was released, but I can now," said Ahmed Kathrada, who was jailed with Mandela. "Madiba starts from the position that everyone is good unless proved otherwise."

Mandela supported the Truth and Reconciliation process led by Archbishop Tutu that convened hearings on crimes committed under apartheid. Through the process, in the interests of a type of "restorative justice," wrongdoers could voluntarily confess to their crimes and seek amnesty, or even forgiveness.

Said Tutu later, "The turmoil and instability that many feared would accompany these crucial events have not occurred. Why?

"Well, first, you have prayed for us and, if miracles had to happen anywhere, South Africa was a prime site for a miracle. And we have been richly blessed to have had at such a critical time in our history a Nelson Mandela. He was imprisoned for twenty-seven years; most expected that when he emerged, he would be riddled with a lust for retribution. But the world has been amazed; instead of spewing calls for revenge, he urged his own people to work for reconciliation—and invited his former jailer to attend his presidential inauguration as a VIP guest.

"Wonderfully, Mr. Mandela has not been the only person committed to forgiveness and reconciliation. Less well-known people (in my theology no one is 'ordinary,' for each one of us is created in the image of God) are the real heroes and heroines of our struggle."

IT's IMPORTANT to remember that apartheid was not just defined by malicious or even criminal acts by individuals, but how people of color were routinely abused. A *Mail & Guardian* writer spoke to that in 1999:

Already, the process of forgetting has begun. Now I find that many no longer remember—or wish to remember— the full extent of the daily horror apartheid caused in the lives of most South Africans.

Not just the almost unspeakable atrocities brought to light by the Truth and Reconciliation Commission, but the small indignities of everyday life—the decayed off-cuts of meat flung, unwrapped, at black customers at a butcher's; the preferential treatment of whites in a post office queue; the delays in paying out old-age pensions to blacks; the man humiliated in front of his small son; the woman addressed as "girl" by a shop assistant half her age who would not allow her to try on clothes before purchasing them; the neglect of black patients in a hospital; the insolence or outright brutality of adolescent white boys in police uniform dealing with the most ordinary of enquiries or terrible of calamities in the lives of blacks; the inferior pay; the charitable dispensing of second-hand clothes or leftover food to the "maid" in the kitchen.

The ANC and the antiapartheid movement had not achieved a military victory over their foes. Despite a desire on the part of many activists to convene tribunals in response to crimes against humanity, like those in Nuremberg that followed World War II to dispense justice onto Nazi war criminals, they lacked the power to do so. (Indeed, even at Nuremberg, scholars note, only a handful of Nazi war criminals were ever jailed or prosecuted and some were even acquitted.)

Mandela, and many of his co-leaders, recognized that a deal would have to be made with "the other side" to win them over to the side of the new "dispensation." They feared that the well-armed and trained former soldiers who fought for the apartheid regime could and would attempt to scuttle the new arrangement and even wage war against it. They were not prepared to fight, much less win such a war.

Psychologist Dr. Judith Rich wrote,

> Looking at the context from which Mandela was shaped, it's hard to imagine that he could have turned out any other way, for he comes out of the African tradition of *Ubuntu*—"I am what I am because of who we all are." If we want to get a clue and catch a glimpse of what's possible for humanity, Nelson Mandela would be a good person to study.

For him to forgive those who imprisoned him for
twenty-seven-and-a-half years, he had to know and
believe something that most of the world has failed to
grasp. For him to emerge from prison and to state: "As
I walked out the door toward my freedom I knew that
if I did not leave all the anger, hatred and bitterness
behind I would still be in prison." He had to be connected
to a belief about the true nature of humanity and thus
his own. He had to be committed to living that belief,
undeterred by the events that had resulted in his imprisonment.

Nevertheless, it was not ideas but deeds that translated forgiveness into practical programs. I remember sitting in the
backyard of Joe Slovo's home in Johannesburg in 1992 as he
explained to me why Mandela was promoting compromises to
entice his former enemies to support, or at least participate in,
what he hoped would become a new government elected by all:
"They have all the arms, the police, and military structures in
place; the ANC does not." Slovo referenced the bloodbath that
followed after the overthrow of President Salvador Allende in
Chile. Mandela knew that revolutions often spark counterrevo-
lutions and so crafted a strategy to co-opt his enemies into the
new order by making them stakeholders.

Mandela also had to reassure his constituency, especially
those who had lost family members, to support compromises
that offended their sense of justice.

He also knew that in the warlike conditions that had prevailed
in South Africa at the time of township uprisings, many blacks

and freedom fighters had also committed crimes. His own wife, Winnie, would later be accused of having a hand in the killing of a young activist and would face charges, though in the end was only convicted on kidnapping.

One especially emotionally searing case put the question of forgiveness in the Mandela model to an agonizing test. It was the story of a young American activist, Amy Biehl, a Mandela supporter who came to South Africa as a voter registration worker, but who was killed during her last few days in the country on August 25, 1993.

Before she traveled to South Africa, she was referred to me for more background and visited with me in my New York office. Amy was an energetic and idealistic person totally committed to supporting the democratic process in South Africa. She had many intelligent questions and impressed me by the seriousness of her interest and depth of commitment.

The next I heard about Amy was that she had been killed—viciously murdered—in a township outside Cape Town by group of black kids who identified with the racialistic antiwhite rhetoric of the Pan Africanist Congress (PAC). The story was widely reported, and eventually the perpetrators were caught. There was no question of their guilt.

Her killers claimed that their crime was fueled by their anti-apartheid outlook and, after being convicted, sought amnesty. Amy's family was asked what they wanted to recommend.

Amy's brother and sisters were initially eager to have her killers punished, but her mother and father considered what Amy would have wanted. They knew she would have supported the principles of the Truth and Reconciliation Commission. And so when the Commission recommended amnesty, the family went along.

In the aftermath of Amy's death, they had started a foundation in her honor to help South African youth.

I followed and reported on this story over the years, but in 2012, Amy's mother, Linda Biehl was in South Africa and I invited her to see the production of *Long Walk to Freedom*. We talked about her journey as we walked down a set with a replica of Nelson Mandela's three-room house on Vilakazi Street in the township of Orlando, later part of Soweto.

She told me what initially inspired her daughter's interest: "Amy really got involved with the issues of South Africa in the '80s as a Stanford student and Nelson Mandela and his story became important to her life and he became her hero. Through various opportunities she ended up here as a Fulbright scholar in 1992 to '93 and in her work and her research she had great opportunities, but she was killed, a few days before she was to come home, by some militant activities prior to the elections.

"People saw her as the oppressor and they were having daily disruptions in the townships just like this. They were toyi-toying, marching down the streets, they were rallying and singing liberation songs and they saw her as the enemy, not knowing who she was, and they were stoning this Coca-Cola truck.

"South Africa went through an amazing process, the Truth and Reconciliation Commission, and it gave people who could possibly apply for amnesty an opportunity to confess to their action and make full disclosure and if the judges of TRC believed them they could be given amnesty and the four young men in Amy's case who had been tried and convicted in a regular court were freed in 1998.

"You have to remember that Nelson Mandela was Amy's hero and what did he represent? He represented total sacrifice to a country, to a people for liberation and he wanted this non-racial democracy. Amy would have been horrified if our family had not supported the process.

"I think when you take a step and make a decision based on your values, you know you're not going to please all the people, so yes, I think we've made many friends. I'm still coming here almost twenty years later with a foundation that is very active in youth development and people support that.

". . . I really love my daughter and I really love what she stood for and I would've been denouncing my own daughter and my family and my late husband, had I not had the capability and the strength to at least support this process. I'm a very private person and it was public event, but I tried to, I think, balance and maintain my privacy. But I want my daughter to be proud of me, too."

As we talk we watch the extras, black men, women, and children, some from the Guguletu township where Amy was killed, getting ready for the next scene.

"And what does this movie, *Long Walk to Freedom*, mean to you, in this context of being in a way dragged into this whole struggle in South Africa and becoming part of it, becoming in some people's eyes a hero?"

"I use Mandela's book, I recommend people who ask me, particularly in the US, 'Well, how can I learn about this?' and I say, 'Read this book.' I've also known the producers and I know this has been a long journey for them. In reality it's been a long walk for this country and it symbolizes a tremendous amount to me, yes it does.

"I think the world maybe needs to hear the story again because some of that antiapartheid activism and history is kind of lost and it should be a symbol to countries around the world going through a lot of upheaval right now. I think it still is. As much as there are still issues remaining, I still think this story is a shining star in many ways to the rest of the world."

Walking in Mandela's footseps, as Linda Biehl is doing, isn't easy. It is among the most difficult of paths, but she shows us it can be done.

GLOBAL

NELSON MANDELA is a South African through and through. He has lived in all the worlds that make up his diverse country with its eleven official languages, many ethnic and tribal groups, and disparate regions and communities. Some who grow up in South Africa still live in rural areas as their ancestors did hundreds of years ago. Others are packed into overcrowded black townships known for their shacks and poverty while still others live affluent lifestyles in plush leafy suburbs.

Mandela has lived as South Africans do, but he is also known globally as a man who belongs to the world. Everyone knows his name, and most value his story. In a country rightfully angry with corruption and self-serving political leaders, his image is untarnished and has only grown in stature over the years. He led South Africa to freedom and equality against impossible odds. His journey personifies the country's journey.

PRODUCER David Thompson, formerly head of BBC Films, has said that Mandela's international status gives them a special responsibility in telling the story:

"Mandela is, rightly, an absolute icon. He is probably the only world leader who has remained completely untarnished, particularly at a time of so much political upheaval across the world. When the changes happen and people get disillusioned, I mean Mandela is the only one whose legacy remains completely intact.

"He is an extraordinary role model for people and he is probably the most famous brand name, after Coca Cola, around the world, and rightly so. He is an incredible inspiration to people—the idea you can actually have radical change and transformation in a country without violence, without revenge, makes him an extraordinary role model and a hero to so many people."

Long Walk to Freedom director Justin Chadwick and I talked about how to free Mandela's story from the mythology. To Chadwick, the story is about a real person struggling for change, and struggling within himself. He said that studying Mandela, the man, not just the icon, has taught him a lot: "It's got to be about the people or the things that you don't know, the things that were happening behind the scenes. It's got to surprise you. You know, there's got to be a humanity to it. Particularly, with a film. You know we can't just polish the veneer of Mandela and what Mandela is. . . . Speaking with the family members was very liberating for me because they said, you know, please treat him as a man."

WHAT IS IT about Mandela that sets him apart?

It's not any one thing—his political achievements, Nobel Prize, outspokenness, humility, courage, AIDS advocacy—but goes deeper. How many who admire him would have made the choices he made, or taken the risks he did—especially when as a lawyer who had "made it," he didn't have to?

And yet, in poll after poll, Mandela is recognized as one of the most popular men in the world, a Man of the Century, afforded the kind of treatment reserved for winners, especially good-looking ones with wide smiles.

The news media coverage worldwide has been largely positive and Mandela has been showered with accolades. His globe trotting, college appearances, and tours have also been widely covered. The Mandela story is one of the few feel-good news stories that keeps giving.

Not everyone is happy with what's been called the global "iconography" that surrounds Mandela.

Frances Lukhele of the University of Swaziland blamed Hollywood for deifying Mandela, in the *Canadian Journal of African Studies*: "Nelson Mandela's global iconography is accompanied by a respectful reluctance to countenance any skepticism with his saintly stature. However, a reading of the 2009 film, *Invictus*, directed by Clint Eastwood, invites an exploration of a dimensionality that has received scant attention, namely, the demonstrable role of the American film industry in the crafting of Mandela's global image."

This article ventured where angels fear to tread in advancing the view that Hollywood has played an inordinate role in the "making" of, or transformation of, post-prison Nelson Mandela into a global hero and secular saint; this process has not been a boon to the average South African Mandela spent nearly three decades to liberate. Indeed, the article argued that the beneficiaries of Mandela's appropriation are the architects of the same, namely, Wall Street, which instrumentalized Mandela to script a jaundiced narrative of South African culture and history.

Critics seem to both admire and sneer at Mandela's fame. A group that keeps track of the net worth of celebrities places

Mandela's at fifteen million dollars. (He had nothing in the bank when he was released from prison in 2000.)

Celebrities seem to love being in his presence, perhaps a symbol of the seriousness and sense of mission missing in their own lives.

I spoke with one of South Africa's best-known writers, Njabulo Ndebele, about this phenomenon. He said, "I think the danger of a celebrity culture in a society that still has so much to do is that it can quickly lapse into simplification and a lack of depth, in a sense that you can solve the deep problems of life through slogans and statements that seem to contain a lot of truth, but in fact don't express the reality that we see out there.

"And I think Madiba tried not to be seen as a celebrity in that sense. I think he always tried to put across the other view, that there is more to me than what you wish to see, and that that is what is important. I think certain societies can play around with celebrities and enjoy it, but they can enjoy it precisely because there is no vulnerability to a sudden collapse, because institutions have been put in place over decades, and sometimes centuries.

"We're struggling to put our feet into the ground, to develop roots. And it is dangerous to pretend that there are roots in the face of notions of perfection that are encapsulated in a celebrity culture."

And yet Mandela is regularly seen, by many, as a saint. So I asked Ndebele, "Do you consider Madiba sanctified?"

And he replied, "I think it is understandable to see him as a saint, because in an imperfect world many of us like to see some models of perfection. But he himself acknowledges that he is not a perfect person. And one can see that when you read about his life—that he has doubts, has experienced pain and suffering, and a good example is when he received the news of the death of his son. It was devastating. And so he reacted as a father, not as a mythical figure. And that made us see him as an ordinary human being."

ANC VETERAN Pallo Jordan was in charge of the ANC's outreach to the press over many years in exile and then on his return to South Africa.

He explained to me why much of the media places Mandela as a global celebrity in a world that is often seen in terms of black and white, good and bad:

"Well the temptation, I think, on the part of the media is always to make someone like that into a celebrity, which I suppose is inevitable, given the environment one lives in. And twentieth-century figures have almost always been transformed, especially by the electronic media, into celebrity figures.

"The temptation is great, but I think that to do so strips Mandela of a lot of what he has going for him, which is that he was in the main a political activist and leader who had a legal profession, not a celebrity.

"He became an iconic figure as a result of his nearly twenty-eight years of imprisonment and that the campaign for the release of South African political prisoners was anchored around his name, which probably contributed to the casting of the person as a celebrity at a certain point.

"Now whether the world needs a figure like that is something we can debate. To make Mandela into that does strip him I think of many dimensions of what he was and what he could be—which is a freedom fighter in the tradition of your Gandhi, of King and earlier freedom fighters.

"Now we might celebrate him, because of his achievements and his deeds, but to reduce him to a celebrity—sort of to make him like Madonna; well that isn't what he is."

Director Justin Chadwick worked hard at not treating Mandela as a celebrity in *Long Walk to Freedom*. He said, "It doesn't feel too reverential or "worthy." We were very, very aware of that in the prep. Anant, Dave, the producers, and Bill [Nicholson, the writer], and I were very, very aware. How do we, how do we get the audience in? And it was through the characters. Through understanding them as three-dimensional, living, breathing characters. Flaws and all."

HUMBLE

IF YOU BELIEVE that Mandela is not a saint (as he says so often he is not), or if you think of him as an ordinary man who has led an extraordinary life (despite not always being one of his own choosing), then you will start to see in him a quality that may seem out of step with his high profile and sometimes vain persona: his humility.

When Anant Singh was pitching him for the rights to make a film based on *Long Walk to Freedom*, Mandela was still in prison. He seemed persuaded by the proposal and knew of Anant's earlier work as an antiapartheid filmmaker. Yet Singh was surprised when he asked in an exchange of letters: "Do you really think anyone will be interested in seeing my story?

Perhaps it was his isolation, his provincialism as someone who hadn't seen the world outside of South Africa, except, briefly, in the 1960s, which made him unable to fully recognize the size of his following and the passion of his supporters. But it was something else, too . . .

For more insight, I spoke with South African writer Nadine Gordimer, winner of the Nobel Prize for Literature, known for the complex characters she invents, and someone who has observed Mandela up close. She spoke to me about why she sees him as an ordinary man. Here's part of our exchange:

"And now in these late years, my connections with Madiba

have been with George [Bizos, his lawyer], George taking me along with him to the circle breakfasts we used to have up until very recently with Madiba.

"Yes. He'd come to breakfast. Because he had his breakfast now—in his later years, when he's not very strong—rather late in the morning. And we'd be invited to the breakfast, and we would feast with him.

"He ate quite a big breakfast. But, you know, he wasn't very mobile anymore by then. So I don't know if he was a big eater otherwise. But as a person, in terms of his conversation and the issues that he addressed, he always seemed to me to be very sharp and clear.

"He was very forthcoming, and obviously if he felt you were a comrade and could be trusted, then he absolutely responded to this in the same warm and trusting way. But of course my most extraordinary experience with him was really a rather sad one.

"But first of all I'll go to the fact that I have a letter from him written on the island, smuggled out I suppose via George. Because he had smuggled in a novel of mine called *The Burger's Daughter*, which indeed looks into how the family of someone who is constantly in and out of jail or in exile or up in the bush—what happens to family life in the younger generation? And he wanted to read this book, and it was smuggled in. He read it then he wrote to me about it. So I have this letter from him which I treasure, and it was my great pleasure and satisfaction that I'd written something worthwhile that he believed had some truth in it.

"Of course, there was great sadness there. We had all seen him coming out of, not Robben Island but that what was it called, that other place . . .

"Victor Verster, yes, out of Verster. There was beautiful Winnie with him, hand in hand. But, of course, when he got home, he found that indeed the relationship with Winnie, the marriage, was just not there. So when I saw him that day he was rather down.

"This wasn't the great Nelson Mandela, but a human being! With all the disappointments and disasters that come to us. And he was broken-hearted."

Gordimer paused, probably out of sensitivity, and wanting to say the right thing.

"I think this was a personal reaction to his feeling of rupture with a woman that he greatly loved. But then I've seen a very nice sequel to this, the way he handled these things. This is only about a year ago, eighteen months perhaps. I was there visiting him with George, I think, or maybe on my own, I can't remember which, and we were having tea or something together, and his daughter came in. Her car arrived and she came in. We greeted one another because she was at school where my son was at school. So I knew her as a schoolgirl. We chatted, and she embraced her father. And he said come, have tea with us and so on. And she said, 'No, I can't 'cause Mama is in the car.' And he said, 'What do you mean in the car? Bring her in.' And she went out, the daughter, and came back with Winnie, and he called Winnie over, and they embraced, and I thought, this is the way to behave, when you've still got family and children, whether they're little or grown-up or whatever they are, you still keep something together. You did have the life together.

"So in a way, I think he developed a very keen sense of the importance of children and family and the like, perhaps because of their absence over so many years."

AMINA CACHALIA was a woman who also experienced that warmth and grew very close to Mandela. After her death in 2012, her daughter reported that Madiba had wanted to marry her, a proposal she had turned down.

Amina chatted with me in what may be her last filmed interview, in August 2012, six months before her memoirs were published, filled with pictures of her as a stunning young woman.

I asked her how they had met. She said she was taken first with his good looks, just as she was about to marry Yusuf Cachalia, an activist in the South African Indian Congress.

"And what was your impression of him, besides his good looks?"

"He looked a very nice guy and I thought to myself, 'Nice chap. I would like to get to know him.'"

"Really? Apparently he felt the same way about you. He was taken with you. He was smitten by you. He seemed to recognize qualities in you that made him feel very comfortable."

"I don't know. But we did become friends. We somehow clicked. We became friends, and then very good friends and our friendship intensified over the years until we lost him, when he went to prison."

"What were the qualities of his leadership or his political involvement that impressed you?"

"You know, when I first met him, he did look like a leader to me. He always had that quality of leadership in the sense of somebody that you look up to, or if he comes into a room, everybody's attention would be on him. That's the sort of aura he had, I think, at that time."

"Well dressed, articulate?"

"He was always well dressed. I had never seen him in just a top and a pants or anything. He was always well dressed."

"Articulate, in terms of his political ideas?"

"I had never been in meetings with Mandela in those years where they discussed ANC or Indian Congress policy or whatever. I was not in that league of leadership. I was an activist. Yusuf, Nelson, Walter, and Dadoo, people like that had those positions. So I was never part of the policy-making of the organization, but I did belong to the Indian Youth Congress later on. And I was always a member of the Indian Congress. We could never become members of the African National Congress in those years because it was a Nationalist organization and they didn't encourage anybody else except black people to become members of the organization."

"That's an interesting evolution, isn't it? That Madiba begins politics with a very Nationalist outlook but broadens his outlook over time."

"I think he probably broadened it very early in life, yes. He did start off with the ANC being a Nationalist organization. I think in his early years, perhaps he didn't trust other organizations or other individuals. . . . There was talk that he once pushed my husband Yusuf off a platform. I was not present at that meeting, so I didn't see it. But when I did ask him about it many years later, 'Why did you do that?' He said, 'No, I didn't push him off. I didn't stop him from talking. I just used some stern words when I talked to him.' That was Madiba's answer.

"That was in the years when he was very Nationalistic-minded. I always said to him, 'Perhaps you didn't trust us those years,' and he would say, 'Well, I didn't trust anybody in those years because they were very difficult years and we had to be very careful about who claimed to be with us in the struggle.'"

I said, "He did become very friendly with many people of all races, people like Joe Slovo, Ruth First. Others seemed to take to him and him to them. He seemed to have an openness to people of other races?"

"He had an openness very early on. Yes, he realized very early on that all these people were absolutely dedicated and sincere in what they were saying and talking about. Especially Joe Slovo. He liked Joe a great deal. I remember when Joe died. He told me that morning when he phoned, saying, 'You must go. Joe has died. Go now. Take Yusuf and go to Joe's house before the crowd of people come. Go and spend some time with the family. Will you go right now?' I said, 'Yes, of course I'll go.'

"So Yusuf and I went immediately to Joe's house. I remember saying to Yusuf then, 'I don't think Madiba realizes how much he is going to miss Joe.'"

"They both had good senses of humor. Wouldn't you agree? Joe and Madiba?" I asked.

"Oh yes, they did. They used to come for lunch together to me in Fordsburg and whilst the talks were on—after he came out of prison and the negotiations were happening. Often they would come together, Joe and him to come and have a bite with me and Yusuf."

Our conversation is chatty, but clearly, on her part, driven by deep affection and loss. Amina's daughter has said that her mother told her that Madiba wanted to be intimate with her even after he married Graça Machel at the age of eighty. Amina reportedly ruled out physical contact. Mandela has not commented on the incident, to my knowledge.

Cachalia herself had experienced house arrest for her anti-apartheid work, she was well known in her community. She knew all the details of Madiba's life, even his favorite foods. There was no pretense between them; they were friends in the struggle and friends in life.

"You enjoyed a very close friendship with Madiba?" I prodded her to tell me more, but she seemed very careful about what to say and how to say it.

"The level of intimacy . . . his ability to talk about everything, that many people would be jealous of."

That's all she would say.

I got the sense there was more she wasn't telling me, but then why would she? We'd only just met.

"Well in the years gone by, when we first got to know him, we had many times together, Yusuf, Nelson, and I. I never found him reserved in a sense. We used to talk and laugh and talk about people and discuss matters and so on. This was not in meetings but in private, when we had lunches together, or gathered together in somebody else's home, or for that matter going to a movie. I did go to a movie with him once or twice. He remembers we went to see *The Ten Commandments*. I can't remember going to see *The Ten Commandments* with him but I remember going to Alexandra Township."

Imagine Nelson Mandela watching *The Ten Commandments*! Years later some of his ardent supporters act as if he wrote them. I clarified: "What I mean is, people see him as this icon, almost as a saint. Whereas he sees himself as an ordinary person or so he says. So a lot of people like him from a distance, as an idea more than as a person. You got to know him as a person."

Amina responded nonchalantly: "I never think of him as an icon. I know everybody does. But to me he is just Nelson Mandela, the guy I knew who has become so famous because of his dedication to the people of South Africa and to the world."

JUST ONE last point on his humility: you can see it in action in this letter he wrote to his friend Fatima Meer, who later became one of his biographers, telling her why he was not interested in writing an autobiography:

> The trouble, of course is that most successful men are prone to some form of vanity. There comes a stage in their lives when they consider it permissible to be ego-tistic and to brag to the public at large about their unique achievements. What a sweet euphemism for self-praise the English language has evolved. Autobiography they choose to call it, where the shortcomings of others are frequently exploited to highlight the praiseworthy accomplishments of the author. I am doubtful if I will ever sit down to scribble my background. I have neither the achievements of which I could boast, nor the skills to do it. If I lived on cane spirit every day of my life I still would not have had the courage to attempt it. I some-times believe that through me Creation intended to give the world the example of a mediocre man in the proper sense of the term. Nothing could tempt me to advertise myself. Had I been in a position to write an autobiog-raphy, its publication would have been delayed until our bones had been laid and perhaps I might have dropped

hints not compatible with my vow. The dead have no worries if the truth and nothing but the whole truth about them, emerged. If the image I have helped to maintain through my perpetual silence was ruined, that would be the affair of posterity, not ours.

In her book, Meer commented, "Remarkable self-assessment in 1971." Five years later, circa 1975, with his prison comrades acting as editors and fact-checkers, and at their request, he wrote the first version of *Long Walk to Freedom*. I saw some of the pages of a version captured by prison guards at the National Archives in Pretoria. I was told it only went up to 1948, and it's rumored that the members of the Communist Party who read it when it was smuggled to London were not happy because it downplayed their role. Whether or not this delayed its publication is not known.

The manuscript was not published until it was revised in 1994, with the help of *Time* editor Richard Stengel, who was hired as a ghostwriter, and with the assistance of historian Gail Gerhart. That book has now become the basis of the film, *Mandela: Long Walk to Freedom*.

INDIGENOUS

THE LAST STOP in Nelson Mandela's triumphant June 1990 tour of the United States—eight cities in eleven days—was in Oakland, California, the onetime home of the Black Panther Party. There many political activists committed to the antiapartheid cause—perhaps because Oakland is as much of a multiracial mosaic as South Africa itself.

Though Mandela's tour had many highlights—with major rallies at New York's Yankee Stadium, the Esplanade in Boston, the old Tiger Stadium in Detroit, the Atlanta stadium, and the Los Angeles Coliseum—all raucous crowds, jammed to the rafters—but the stop in Oakland, the last of the trip, was the most energetic. There were large peoples' choirs, and singers like Bonnie Raitt and Bernice Reagon of Sweet Honey in the Rock. A seventy-year-old Nelson Mandela was trying to keep up after finishing an exhausting cross-country tour in a land that was not his own.

There was stunning oratory that afternoon: the local black Congressman Ron Dellums, who led the fight for sanctions against South Africa on the Hill brought cheers of joy from the crowd with his eloquence.

The buildup to the event started at the airport, where hardcore activists had welcomed Madiba. Among them was a small group of Native Americans who brought him a special gift along with a letter that they had previously sent but didn't know if he had received. They told me they saw him not just as a freedom fighter, but as a fellow "tribal person," and wanted to share that message of shared identity.

Politicians regularly receive presents from well wishers that their aides usually pack away. But in this case, Mandela received their gesture and message of solidarity personally, which he demonstrated by interrupting his planned remarks at Oakland Coliseum—calling for sanctions on South Africa to remain in place until a date for elections was set—by giving the Native Americans in the audience a shout-out. He said he was very moved by their gift and remarks, and promised to return to America to visit native reservations. This pledge distressed his ANC handlers, who recognized that Mandela was now interfering in America's internal affairs; they knew that no plans for such a trip had been made and believed none would be.

I was there covering the event for a film called *Mandela in America*. Madiba's remarks struck me as a deviation from the script that these events normally followed. Later, I tracked down two of the women who were in that delegation of Native Americans; one of them told me about their reaction to the unexpected acknowledgment:

"We were thrilled to be there and listened carefully to his remarks. And then suddenly I realized he was talking about us, about indigenous people. Oh, my God."

She said they began weeping at the way he showed an affinity with their backgrounds.

"He was talking about us, our people," the other woman seconded, also choking up with emotion. I don't remember their names, but I haven't forgotten their passion, or how touched Mandela was to be treated as an indigenous leader, as part of a tribe and a clan, connecting him to, reminding him of, his upbringing and culture.

This isn't something that is usually recognized as important by many of the people who salute him for his work in the struggle as an ANC leader and president. Mandela always reached out to traditional leaders in South Africa whom he invited to his events and consulted with politically. Moreover, he always saw himself as a "country boy," meaning someone whose original culture was tribal.

HIS FORMALITY, what is sometimes confused with remoteness, has its origins in his traditional upbringing, said Mac Maharaj, who spent many years with him in prison:

"I have asked him in retirement, 'Madiba, did you ever joke, laugh, pull pranks with your mum and your family and tease?' He says, 'No, we don't do that. We don't do that.'

"I wanted to know whether his mum had embraced him and kissed him. 'No, she had simply said, "Young boy be strong," and it literally translates to say that, "When we are born, our skull bones are still soft, and when those begin to get harder and settle, that's what you call bracing yourself."'

"So I'm saying that Madiba's upbringing was an intimate, warm, and secure one. But the levels of showing intimacy with each other had very strict rules within the family that he grew up in and that put a certain distance there. . . . So in that upbringing, there is also a remoteness."

Mandela was raised in the traditional culture of the Xhosa tribe, who, according to travel writer Henk Aartsma,

[A]lso belonged to the Nguni speaking tribes who moved into South Africa during the great southern migration.

The very first Xhosa tribes arrived on the scene in South Africa in the 14th century, spearheading the Great Southern Migration ahead of the Zulu tribes.

Originally they settled in the coastal region from the Mtamvuna River near Port St. Johns in KwaZulu-Natal to the Great Fish River in the Eastern Cape. . . .

Comprising approximately 8 million people, 18% of the total South African population, the amaXhosa (Xhosa nation) form the second largest black nation in South Africa. It's with the amaXhosa where the struggle for freedom from apartheid had its roots with world icons like Nelson Mandela and Steve Biko.

Nelson Mandela was born at Mvezo, a tiny village on the banks of the Mbashe River, in the district of Mthatha, the capital of the Transkei, which is 800 miles east of Cape Town, 550 miles south of Johannesburg, and in between the Kei River and the Natal border. He was given the name "Rolihlahla" at birth by his father on July 18, 1918. It translates literally to "pulling the branch of a tree" or "trouble maker." A teacher, Miss Mdingane, gave him the name Nelson in line with the common practice of giving African children English names.

His father, Gadla Henry Mphakanyiswa, was confirmed as chief of Mvezo by the king of the Thembu tribe. Mandela's father had four wives, the third was Mandela's mother. Mandela is the youngest of his father's four sons, and he also had three sisters.

The Xhosa are proud people who believe in the importance

of laws, education, and courtesy. Every individual knew his or her place. They acquired knowledge through observation. In his household, he never asked his parents a question, he had to learn himself by watching. There were many stories passed on from generation to generation depicting Xhosa warriors. At age sixteen, in accordance with Xhosa tradition, Mandela was circumcised in an initiation ceremony performed by an *ingcibi*, a medicine man.

DURING HIS first speech in Cape Town after being released from prison, Mandela signaled respect for indigenous people, saying, "I greet the traditional leaders of our country. Many among you continue to walk in the footsteps of great heroes like Hintsa and Sekhukhuni."

After he grew older and retired from politics, he moved back to the Eastern Cape, living in a house in Qunu modeled exactly after the home the prison authorities gave him at Victor Verster prison, his first taste of freedom, even while he was still behind bars. He liked the house, even after he learned that the authorities planted microphones all through it, and then decided to rebuild it as his final place of residence.

In 2007, the *Mail & Guardian* reported:

> Former South African President Nelson Mandela beamed on as he watched his grandson reclaim a traditional leadership post that Mandela had renounced decades ago to become a lawyer and dedicate his life to fighting apartheid.
>
> Mandla Mandela, 32, was draped in a lion skin, the symbol of royalty, and officially installed as head of the

Mvezo Traditional Council by the king of the AbaTh-
embu, Zwelibanzi Dalindyebo, one of six kings of the
Xhosa people.

Mandla, who became quite controversial in his own right,
sought to carry on the Mandela family tradition. Mandela once
said, upon returning to the place of his birth, "There is nothing
like returning to a place that remains unchanged to find the
ways in which you yourself have been altered." On the day of his
grandson's appointment, Mandela was heard to say, "Now I can
die in peace."

JAILED

I AM HOLDING a key, one of those old fashioned metal ones that you keep on a chain with a long stem. It's a key that was used to open and reopen cells in South Africa's most draconian penitentiary, the maximum security unit built in 1961 on windswept Robben Island, named after the seals that congregate there on a relatively small spit of land off the coast of Cape Town.*

Earlier in the country's history, Robben Island was populated by people with leprosy, as well as the mentally and chronically ill. A museum exhibit there explains, "People lived on Robben Island many thousands of years ago, when the sea channel between the Island and the Cape mainland was not covered with water. Since the Dutch settled at the Cape in the mid-1600s, Robben Island has been used primarily as a prison. Indigenous African leaders, Muslim leaders from the East Indies, Dutch and British soldiers and civilians, women, and antiapartheid activists, including South Africa's first democratic president, Nelson Rolihlahla Mandela and the founding leader of the Pan Africanist Congress, Robert Mangaliso Sobukwe, were all imprisoned on the island."

Robben Island's role as a political prison made it infamous around the world even before the modern democratic era, prior to its closure and transformation into a UNESCO World Heritage

---

* Robben is the Dutch word for seal.

site and tourist attraction. When I first visited the prison in 1995, a year after Mandela became president, it was to film a reunion organized to promote reconciliation. As an American television producer who had visited and reported on American prisons over the years, I couldn't help but notice that our maximum security prisons seem far more brutal and repressive because prisoners are confined to their cells for twenty-three hours a day, solitary confinement over long periods is common, and, especially at the most modern, high-tech prisons like Guantánamo, other forms of torture are also commonly used.

The more than ten thousand days across nearly twenty-eight years that Nelson Mandela spent behind bars—eighteen on Robben Island, the rest in other institutions—were not a picnic. Prisoners broke rocks in a lime quarry and were segregated like in society at large. Political prisoners were only allowed limited visits, and initially, could only receive one letter per prisoner every six months. The mail was censored and all contacts were monitored, especially for so-called D-Group offenders—the political leaders—including Mandela.

South African citizens who grew up opposed to the government learned to cope with and subvert rules designed to insure apartheid separation and to dampen dissent. One of Mandela's closest comrades in prison, Ahmed Kathrada, explained to me how he and his comrades were always searching for ways to turn the system to their advantage: "It was regimentation in every aspect of our lives. And when we landed in prison, it was even more regimented of course."

I asked Kathy, "Yet isn't it true, as somebody told me the other day (who was in the prison that you were in) that Madiba once said he wished the days were longer, because he had so much to do? Was he really that organized, that disciplined? Was he able to deal with prison so well that he turned it into a positive experience?"

"Well, what Madiba has frequently said is that he misses prison because it gave him time to think, which did not happen when he was with all of us together. And, eventually when they separated him from us at Pollsmoor, that is when he had a lot of time to think. And that is when he took this very important decision, to talk to the other side."

The prisoners resisted, or tried to resist, the harsh rules and regulations. At the same time, they sought to use the time to improve themselves and each other. The older men taught the younger men. There were classes and study sessions. Mandela played teacher and student, and cheerleader for all of the men, including the guards, to engage in what were called "studies." Mandela studied at the University of London via correspondence, and, though he was already credentialed and practicing as a lawyer, he eventually received a degree of bachelor of laws from the University of South Africa in 1989. The prison would later be dubbed "Robben Island University" because it had been transformed into a place of learning and instruction.

ANC leader Pallo Jordan explained to me, "I think many of the people who went through the Robben Island experience referred to it as like a university, because you had people, political prisoners who came to the island, who were virtually illiterate. The incumbent president being a case in point.

"Jacob Zuma arrived on the island with something like five years of primary school education on the outside. And he literally learned to read and write, and to master the English language, on Robben Island. And look where he is today.

"Many others came there with no formal education whatsoever. And were literally taught from primary school upwards. Others arrived on the island and took university courses by correspondence, and came out with degrees."

What the politically conscious prisoners missed most, Ahmed Kathrada told me, was news of the struggle. They bartered for newspapers with corrupt guards. They had black maids who cleaned the warders' quarters steal newspapers for them. At one point, he said, they even had an illegal radio to hear news reports.

Many of the prisoners had escape fantasies and even some plans. In 1969, one such plot was infiltrated by government agents. Later, another one involving a helicopter was rejected by the ANC in Lusaka. The ANC leaders were cautious, fearing prisoners would be shot if caught.

Mandela spent hours reading works by Leo Tolstoy and Winston Churchill, a history of the Boer War, political biographies. Besides learning Afrikaans, he studied religions, including Islam, and attended Christian services even though he was never religious.

NOT ALL the Robben Island prisoners got along. Mandela frequently quarreled over political issues with Govan Mbeki, who was considered a hardline Stalinist. (Interestingly, it would be Govan's son, Thabo, who would follow Mandela as president of the nation, after first serving as Mandela's deputy president. Thabo once compared himself to a "Thatcherite" and would remain hostile to those on his Left while in office. He was largely a realist and pragmatist.)

Mandela speaks with fellow prisoner Walter Sisulu in a rare photo in the yard outside his cell on Robben Island in 1964.

In 1975, a secret memorandum on ANC "discord" was smuggled out of Robben Island and appears in a scholarly collection of documents. The memo acknowledged that the ANC ran "efficient clandestine communications channels," and it revealed disagreements within the decision-making body called "the High Organ," which included Mandela. Some of the issues seemed personal and involved questioning whether there was sufficient self-criticism on the part of the leaders, including Madiba. A review by prisoners found that all the "High Organ men were primarily responsible for disunity." When there was a "report back" to all the prisoners on the issues, the document concluded, "By an overwhelming majority, the meeting reaffirmed Madiba's leadership of the Congress Movement on Robben Island prison."

WHAT DID Mandela expect when he first arrived on the island? I spoke to his lawyer, George Bizos, who was one of his first visitors:

"The title of his book, *Long Walk to Freedom*, comes from a saying that included the idea that the road to freedom passes through the jail. Although he was encouraged by what was happening with the decolonization process in the rest of Africa, he was sufficiently well informed and smart enough to know that the whites here would try and string it out for as long as possible. So time in jail was to be expected. And the one thing that he didn't do was to express a feeling of despair, because that would have been counterproductive to the people on the outside who remained relatively free, whom he wanted to continue the struggle."

When Bizos was questioned for the O'Malley Archives, an online archive hosted by the Nelson Mandela Centre of Memory, he was asked, "You saw him in prison. He somehow elicited a special kind of treatment from the warders. Do you have any recollections or anecdotes on that?"

Bizos responded: "On my first visit, in the middle of winter, he was brought to the consulting room where I was waiting. There were eight warders with him, two in front, two at the back, two on each side. Prisoners do not usually set the pace at which they move with their warders. But it was quite obvious that he was doing so—from the open van, right up to the little verandah of the consulting rooms. I stepped down, past the two in front, and embraced him, and said, 'Hello.' He returned the greeting, and immediately asked, 'How's Zami?'—which is, 'How is Winnie?' And he then pulled himself back and said, 'George, I'm sorry, I have not introduced you to my guard of honor.' And then proceeded to introduce each one of the warders by name. Now the warders were absolutely amazed. I think that this was the first time that they saw a white man, and particularly a lawyer, I suppose, coming and embracing a black man. They were absolutely stunned, and they actually behaved like a guard of honor. They respectfully shook my hand. And there was a lot of evidence that he was treated special, which I knew was to my advantage as well. As a visitor, if you visited Mandela, you were invited to lunch at the officers club on the island, where they lived well with seafood cocktail and grilled lobsters. If you visited anyone else, you were left to your own devices, and the only place where you could have lunch was at the warders canteen, where the specialty was liver hamburgers."

CHRISTO BRAND, one of several Afrikaner warders, or guards, who interacted with Mandela, told me how Mandela regarded his time in prison after hard labor stopped in 1977:

"His days were too short in prison. A lot of days he was studying, he was busy with his garden, everything, the days was too
short in prison for him. . . . When we open [the cells] in the
morning, he'd go and clean the outside toilets and things. And
then he will go to his garden, attend to his garden. Then he will
sit with his studies. Then [at] twelve o'clock we must call him into
his cell. He will just eat his food, put some away for tonight, and
will start studying again. Then we take him out for work a little bit, for an hour in the garden, then his days were really too
short. . . . He had a schedule. Five o'clock in the morning, up. . . .
Physical exercises, push-ups, sit-ups—everything in his cell till
we open up, then he'll take a jog. . . . Tennis certain days, making
sure he plays tennis, also table tennis. He will play sport. Even to
the others, put up teams and thing—they must play sport. They
must keep them[selves] physically fit, even though the limestone
[is] very hard work."

ANOTHER PART of his "work" in prison involved letters to friends
and family members, counseling them about educational issues.
He took his responsibilities as a father seriously, often scolding
his kids for not being ambitious enough or working hard enough
at their studies. Fatima Meer's authorized biography, *Higher than
Hope*, reprints some of this moving correspondence, showing
how Mandela—known to his kids as *Tata*—played taskmaster,
alternating criticism and praise, while always offering advice.

At the same time, he often confessed in his letters to feelings
of guilt for not being able to be there for the children. In some
letters, Mandela wrote about his dreams and his sense of loss.
Some of his children may have resented his long-distance coun-

seling of them and felt unable to meet his standards. There was tension sometimes in their relationships.

MANDELA NOT only influenced family members. Prison guard Christo Brand has said that Mandela changed him. Actor Jamie Bartlett, who plays James Gregory, another guard that Mandela befriended, told me the same thing based on Gregory's own book, *Goodbye, Bafana: Nelson Mandela, My Prisoner, My Friend*, his account of his life as a Robben Island prison guard.

"There were many resonant points in their relationship," says Bartlett of the bond that came to be between Mandela and guard Gregory.

"He grew to love Mandela very, very deeply. He grew to respect him. He grew to understand his politics. Mandela changed Gregory. He was a catalyst for massive change in Gregory's outlook. But I don't want to take away from the fact that Gregory was an asshole who worked for the state. And he was intellectually limited. And his movement, although big, was limited by the fact that the nut that you started with didn't really—couldn't really—go that far. Yet he did go to the library and do research, and started to understand something about what Mandela was saying with his politics."

I asked, "Isn't the Gregory relationship sort of an example of how Madiba reached all kinds of people who first feared him and then came to respect him?"

"Absolutely. It's resonant in all of them. And it's a very good and typical example of how this man reached out and touched all kinds of people."

ZELDA LA GRANGE is another one. She was a young Afrikaner woman from Pretoria who had been in the typing pool in the office of the presidency. Mandela offered her a position as a secretary and, later, as a personal assistant post-presidential office. She told me how his prison routine carried over into his work habits during his presidency, how he paced himself, and even what he ate:

"His stamina is from living the healthy lifestyle that he has led over the years. As a boxer—you know how strict boxer training is—and then during his imprisonment, he also exercised every day. During his presidency, he had to be woken when on his overseas visits, whenever we travelled he needed to be woken up at a certain time for him to exercise. Regardless of where we were in the world, there always had to be time for him to exercise. And I think we as young people underestimate now what that means later in life, but clearly he is proof of that. His eating habits are just exceptionally healthy."

"What does he eat?" I prodded.

"He has a very good breakfast—mixtures of cereals and cooked breakfasts, fruit every day. He has vegetables, protein every day. He doesn't snack in-between. He doesn't take MSG like we do, no fast food. I have never seen him eating fast food.

"Big Mac?"

"Never!"

"Egg McMuffin?"

"Never! Never! And I can also say that I have never had any McDonald's myself. But also that he has never had fast food in his life."

MANDELA'S GHOSTWRITER Richard Stengel wrote: "Over and over, though, I used to ask him how prison had changed him. How was the man who came out in 1990 different from the man who entered in 1962? This question annoyed him. He either ignored it, went straight to a policy answer, or denied the premise. Finally, one day, he said to me in exasperation, 'I came out mature.'

"To me, those four words are the deepest clue to who Nelson Mandela is and what he learned. Because that sensitive, emotional young man did not go away! He is still inside the Nelson Mandela we see today. By maturity, he meant that he learned to control those more youthful impulses, not that he was no longer stung or hurt or angry. It is not that you always know what to do or how to do it, it is that you are able to tamp down the emotions and anxieties that get in the way of seeing the world as it is. You can see through them, and that will see you through.

"At the same time, he realized that not everyone can be Nelson Mandela. Prison steeled him, but it broke many others. Understanding that made him more empathetic, not less."

MANDELA SPENT many long hours in prison reading, writing, and thinking about the future. He felt convinced he would see freedom in his lifetime and became absorbed in cultivating his adversaries and leading his comrades by example.

He moved so slowly at times that he drove the people closest to him crazy. Herman Animba Toivo Ja Toivo, a Namibian leader of the South West Africa People's Organization (SWAPO) liberation movement, used to play chess with him.

"I couldn't take it," Toivo told me in 1995. "Sometimes he

would only make one move in a day. I was too impatient to sit with him. He would always win."

Mandela was always solicitous of prominent visitors, like the members of the multinational Commonwealth "Eminent Persons Group" who visited him in the mid-1980s. Lord Barber of Standard Bank was Margaret Thatcher's nominee to the group, and he is credited as being the one who persuaded P. W. Botha to see him and his colleagues.

According to biographer Anthony Sampson, the government came to consider Mandela more dangerous in prison than out.

Sampson recounted, "All the members of the Eminent Persons Group were surprised by Mandela's mellowness, good judgment, and humor, [but] perhaps most of all Lord Barber, who exchanged stories with Mandela about his own escape from a Russian prisoner of war camp about which he had written. 'Lord Barber,' said Mandela, 'send me a copy [of the writing]. That could be very useful.'"

MANDELA KEPT track of all of his visits and visitors. They were often scribbled on monthly calendars. He noted events, as on November 28, 1989, "Mary Benson's birthday"; referring to his friend Mary, a writer and activist; on December 13, 1989, "Met State President F. W. de Klerk for 2 hrs, 55 minutes." He was very precise. It was never "around 3 hours." On the last day of that year, he noted his weight, blood pressure, and trouser size (87 R, 34 R). He also noted his pants style, 8127.

Ramphela Mamphele, the doctor, economist, one-time girlfriend of Steve Biko, and in 2013 a political candidate of her own Agang Party challenging the ANC, told me about her first visit to see Mandela in Pollsmoor Prison. Her memories were vivid and exact: "It was a very emotional meeting for me because, having read about him and heard about him as a student activist, to actually see the man himself walk into the room where I was waiting wearing a very properly pressed khaki outfit, which could've been a smart casual outfit anywhere in the world, but these were prison clothes actually. But the way he was carrying himself; tall, proud, very confident and with a very cordial relationship with his jailers whom one could regard as his bodyguards. So that was the first encounter; it was a Sunday morning in July 1988." She also told me Mandela asked her to organize an independent advisory group of top academics and experts to help plan the transition, but that the ANC killed the idea.

In the film *Long Walk to Freedom*, there is a scene of a prison visit from his daughter Zindzi. She shows him a campaign button that says, "Free Mandela." His reaction is to ask about the other political prisoners. Her response is, "Tata, there is not enough room on the badge!"

KAFKAESQUE

FRANZ KAFKA'S stories are recognizable for the way they describe individuals caught up in faceless bureaucracies that operate according to arbitrary laws that deprive people of their rights. Kafka never wrote about apartheid South Africa, but his worldview anticipated some of the worst features of countries whose byzantine laws routinely violate human rights.

It was these laws that young lawyers like Nelson Mandela and Oliver Tambo confronted. Apartheid justified itself with the power of law. In many cases, the architects of the system were lawyers who believed in institutionalizing racism through legislation that was easy to pass because nonwhites could not vote in South Africa. The white Nationalist government elected in 1948 started using their monopoly on power to legalize their prejudices and social theories.

These laws also had another, equally important rationale that much of the foreign media often miss: the laws were not just racial or punitive but part of a system of labor domination that regulated blacks as workers, including how and where they could live, not merely to oppress them, but also to use them and the work they did.

RACIAL CLASSIFICATION laws in South Africa were especially bizarre, with some members of the same family classified differently. A "pencil test" was used to assess how kinky a person's hair was. Noses were measured. Japanese people were considered honorary whites, while the Chinese were deemed black.

Among the laws:

Prohibition of Mixed Marriages Act, Act No. 55 (1949): Prohibited marriages between white people and people of other races. Between 1946 and the enactment of this law, only seventy-five mixed marriages had been recorded, compared with some 28,000 white marriages.

Immorality Amendment Act, Act No. 21 (1950; amended in 1957 as the Immorality Act, Act No. 23, later named the Sexuality Offences Act): Prohibited adultery, attempted adultery, or related immoral acts (extramarital sex) between white and any nonwhite people. An update to a 1927 law that prohibited these acts between white and black people only.

Population Registration Act, Act No. 30 (1950): Led to the creation of a national register in which every person's race was recorded. In disputed cases, a Race Classification Board made the final decision on what a person's race was.

Group Areas Act, Act No. 41 (1950): Forced physical separation by race through the creation of different residential areas for different races. Led to the forced removal of people living in "wrong" areas—for example, colored people (i.e., neither black nor white) living in District Six in Cape Town.

Suppression of Communism Act, Act No. 44 (1950): Outlawed Communism and the Community Party in South Africa. Communism was defined so broadly that it covered any call for radical change. Communists could be banned from participating in a political organization and restricted to a particular area.

Mandela in his Mandela & Tambo law office. JURGEN SCHADEBERG

Native Building Workers Act, Act No. 27 (1951): Allowed black people to be trained as artisans in the building trade, something previously reserved for whites only, but they had to work within an area designated for blacks. It was a criminal offense for a black person to perform any skilled work in urban areas except in those sections designated for black occupation.

Separate Representation of Voters Act, Act No. 46 (1951): Together with the 1956 amendment, this act led to the removal of colored people from the common voters' roll.

A Stanford University project on the use of technology to further the apartheid regime in South Africa explained:

"Race laws touched every aspect of social life, including a prohibition of marriage between nonwhites and whites, and the sanctioning of 'white-only' jobs. In 1950, the Population Registration Act required that all South Africans be racially classified into one of three categories: white, black (African), or colored (of mixed descent). The colored category included major subgroups of Indians and Asians. Classification into these categories was based on appearance, social acceptance, and descent.

"For example, a white person was defined as 'in appearance obviously a white person or generally accepted as a white person.' A person could not be considered white if one of his or her parents were nonwhite. The determination that a person was 'obviously white' would take into account 'his habits, education, and speech and deportment and demeanor.' A black person would be of or accepted as a member of an African tribe or race, and a colored person is one that is not black or white.

"The Department of Home Affairs (a government bureau) was responsible for the classification of the citizenry. Noncompliance with the race laws were dealt with harshly. All blacks were required to carry 'pass books' containing fingerprints, photo, and information on access to nonblack areas."

These laws infuriated the majority of the country's people and sparked a Defiance Campaign, during which Africans, Indians, and others deprived of their rights rallied and mounted mass civil disobedience protests, including "stay aways" from work and strikes. Nelson Mandela became the volunteer in chief for that campaign.

The journalist who would become his biographer, Anthony Sampson, noted that Mandela's politics were formed in that period:

> The aggression, at that time, was considerable, yes. The aggression pressed him into politics. Of course, the city life made him feel that he was part of a much larger society [of people] who were suffering in a way that he hadn't properly comprehended, or hadn't felt before he came to Johannesburg. So it was a combination of the personal humiliations, which were almost visible every day, together with the awareness of being part of this bigger scene.
>
> For the first years of apartheid, from '48, certainly, until the Defiance Campaign began in '52, and quite a lot after that, it wasn't taken all that seriously. There was an expectation that the whole thing was not going to work. It would crumble. That part of it, of course, was simply an extension of traditional segregation, and the world trend was against that.

In that period, as the laws became more repressive, it seemed risky that Mandela would team up with his friend Oliver Tambo and open a law office. They would use the law to fight the law. He wrote about it later in *Long Walk to Freedom*: "We were not the only African lawyers in South Africa, but we were the only firm of African lawyers. . . . To reach our offices each morning, we had to move through a crowd of people in the corridors, and in our small waiting room. Africans were desperate for legal help."

The Kafkaesque apartheid laws may have been bad for the country, but they were good for the firm of Mandela and Tambo in Chancellor House, on Fox Street, in central Johannesburg; they put the attorneys on the map—conveniently, just across the street from the Magistrates Court—and elevated their role in the larger freedom fight.

According to Oliver Tambo's son, Dali, "Nelson helped bring in the clients, but Oliver did most of the work."

As Kgalema Motlanthe explained: "Madiba told me, 'Oliver was by far a better lawyer than I was. However, from the point of view of the finances of this firm, Oliver was hopeless.' When I asked him, 'Why?,' this was Madiba's answer: 'Because Oliver would never ever interrupt a client.'

"Once a client walked in, Oliver would just take notes and only ask questions at the end. But Madiba understood that Africans never get straight to the point; they always have lengthy preambles. So he says a man would walk into the office and start telling him, 'It was over the Easter weekend and my uncle was also there, the entire clan was there,' and start telling him the names of each one and so on. And so Madiba would say, 'Thank you very much. We will make time, and you will tell me all about this some

another time. How can I be of help to you now?' And then, only
then, would the client say, 'Well, we took a decision to purchase
a piece of land and we would like you to help us with the convey-
ance and ensuring that we get the title deeds for it.' And so he
would see thirty clients and Oliver would see twelve clients."

GEORGE BIZOS, who went to law school with Mandela and
became one of the country's most famous defense lawyers, as
well as Madiba's personal attorney, told me of the bravery and
dedication that Mandela and Tambo showed in setting up their
firm and serving their clients the way they did: "They would later
become famous as politicians fighting to bring down apartheid,
but they started as advocates working for justice on behalf of
individuals who were being trampled by the legalistic apparatus
of a state machine. They saw how the personal became the political, and why the people could be united against the regime."

LOVE AND LOSS

IT HAS BEEN said that Mandela loved women, and that women loved him. He was tall, handsome, well dressed, and he lit up every room he entered. Yet he was also respectful and didn't speak down to females. He married three times, and it's rumored that he proposed to others.

But not all of his relationships with women were of a romantic nature. One of the women he worked alongside and grew close to was Ruth First, a journalist and activist who became Joe Slovo's wife. Mandela wrote movingly about her in his book *In His Own Words*, after she was killed by a letter bomb that was sent to her in Mozambique by members of the South African secret police. The bomb also injured ANC leader Pallo Jordan.

He wrote:

> Ruth engaged in intense debate while we were at Wits University together; who uncompromisingly broke with the privilege of her wealthy background; who readily crossed the racial barrier that so few whites were, or still are, able to cross; a woman whose passion and compassion enabled others, including those from liberal and conservative perspectives, to play their part.
>
> It is a small consolation that her memory lives beyond the grave, that her freedom of spirit infuses many com-

mitted to an open society, rigorous intellectual thought, courage and principled action.

ONE OF THE women Mandela came to know well from her twenty-first birthday, Amina Cachalia, told her daughter before her death that he told her he wanted to marry her. Her first memory was of his "huge frame and big hands," and humility. She was gorgeous, and she was struck by his formidable handsome look.

Nelson Mandela was widely considered to be a womanizer. He himself admitted he had been sexist, while at the same time also seeking a role as a family man, a father, and a husband. In his final book, *Conversations with Myself*, he confessed to some of these flaws. In a review, the *Independent* (London) noted, "Before he went to prison, he was a legendary womanizer, particularly after he was married. He shamefully neglected his children, may or may not have beaten his wife (he denies the rumours, saying she attacked him with a red-hot poker), was vain, selfish . . ."

In *Young Mandela*, a biography authorized by Mandela's foundation, author David James Smith wrote:

> He was tall, handsome and thin—thanks to the running and boxing which he took up at university. He was a born charmer with natural charisma. Inevitably, women fell at his feet.
>
> The one he married when he was 26, Evelyn, was almost written out of his story in later years. They had two sons and two daughters and he acquired his first home in Orlando East, a district of Soweto.
>
> Evelyn began to complain of his friendships with

other pretty women, including Ruth Mompati, his law firm secretary, whom he sometimes brought home after work and who would follow him into the bedroom, possibly not to take dictation. . . . There were other lady friends from the African National Congress, to whom he devoted nearly all his leisure.

Justin Cartwright, the *Observer*'s reviewer of *Young Mandela*, went further: "David James Smith finds evidence that Mandela was in many ways a traditional African, who regarded himself as head of the family and expected to be obeyed. This is hardly a surprise. He also produces evidence that Mandela may sometimes have hit his first wife, Evelyn, and that he had a child by another woman. Evelyn retired eventually to the Transkei and lived on in embittered silence, although she talked to an earlier Mandela biographer, Fatima Meer, saying that Nelson was the only man she had ever loved and that he was a wonderful father."

Even as Cartwright sits in judgment on Mandela, he has concluded fairly: "The greatness of Mandela is not diminished by his adulteries and his desertions or his inability to demonstrate affection for his children. It lies in his unshakable resolve to produce a fair and humane society for all in South Africa, a legacy now under threat."

In *Mandela: The Authorized Portrait*, Ruth Mompati, the law firm secretary referenced by Smith, also emphasized his strengths and does not talk about any intimate relationship with her boss. "I had utter respect for him because he had respect for the three of us secretaries, and for the articled clerks, and the messenger, who was a friend because he belonged to his boxers' stable. You could see the type of person he was—he was able to relate to people with respect. . . . He listened. He didn't talk down to women; he treated them as if they mattered."

Some of the claims about Mandela's infatuations with women seem bizarre. The *Mail* (London) carried this headline: "Nelson Mandela's secret love . . . for Rolling Stone Ronnie Wood's mother-in-law. Rachel Lundell, mother of Jo Wood, was 16 when Mandela pledged his love."

Simon Trump reported, in March 2013,

> Rachel, now 78 and living in Devon, had just finished convent school in 1951. She was working in her aunt's fruit store and cafe after having second thoughts about life as a nun. . . . "One day [Nelson Mandela] came in and I served him as usual but after he left, I noticed there was a letter on the counter addressed to me. I opened it and there was yards and yards of it. It started off lovey-dovey enough but before long it had turned into something of a political missive all about how he was going to free the blacks in our country. Not very romantic, really. Then, Gertie came in and saw me reading the letter. She asked who it was from and I told her. She snatched it out of my hands and threw it on the fire, saying I wasn't going to be going out with any black men." . . . Rachel never saw Mandela again.

MANDELA'S GREAT love and, perhaps greatest lust, was for the woman who became his second wife, born Nomzamo Winfreda Zanyiwe Madikizela but later known worldwide just as Winnie

Madikizela. She was a twenty-two-year-old social worker from Pondoland, daughter of a headmaster, and sixteen years Mandela's junior, sweeping him away with her beauty, charisma, sensibility, and evolving militancy. As a child, she had been rebellious and occasionally violent, wrote biographer Anthony Sampson.

Winnie's father opposed the marriage, saying Mandela was already married to the struggle. Soon, she would join it. Their love affair was like a fairytale. Nelson and Winnie became the movement's royalty, known for "American-style" glamor. "Winnie was soon developing her own sense of theater and would soon appear as the Amazon of the revolution," wrote Sampson. Not surprisingly, their relationship is the centerpiece of the film *Mandela: Long Walk to Freedom*.

Naomie Harris, an English actor who starred in *Skyfall* and *The First Grader*, plays Winnie. Her research was thorough and she came to see many sides to an often demonized woman. At the same time, she said, there were personal reasons that made it initially hard for her to get into her character: "I think the hardest thing for me has been that I don't have hatred and bitterness in my life, you know. There are things that I'm definitely angry about, but [Winnie's] bitterness, for me, is about sustained hatred, and I don't have hatred, and I don't have bitterness. So to try and get in touch with those kinds of emotions, the emotions that one tries to stay away from in life, has been really challenging. I found that I really struggled in the beginning to get in touch with that."

Explained screenwriter William Nicholson: "This is a movie, and it's therefore about people. It's actually about a man and a woman, and wonderfully the two stories do tell the history. The

stories of Mandela and of Winnie do also give you the story of
what was happening to the country through this period—all of
the emotional, psychological, political stresses. I decided that
the way to tell the [larger] story was through the relationship of
these two."

Before they married, Mandela reached out to his friend Fatima
Meer and her husband Ismail, asking them to take Winnie under
their wing. Fatima recalled, "That first time that we met Winnie,
we didn't think that she was his beloved. . . . We had a call from
Nelson asking us to go to the station and pick up Miss Madikizela. We thought nothing of that request. We thought it must be
a relative or just somebody whom we have to pick up. At the station we met this absolutely vivacious, beautiful young woman,
and we took her home.

"But I must say I was not very impressed with Winnie. I didn't
see her as in my league—snobbish or whatever you call it. I
handed her over to my niece, who was also staying with us at
the time. Winnie spent a week or two weeks—I don't remember
exactly how long. But one day I found her perusing through some
photographs which she took out of her handbag, and they were
the photographs of Nelson in various postures and poses, and
the boxing one dominated that portfolio. Then I realized that
something was cooking between her and Nelson."

Meer told a story about what sold Winnie on Nelson. The two
of them were in a boisterous nightclub one night when it was
invaded by gangsters. Both of them hid under a table until Mandela put his arm around her and escorted her out. She saw that as
a sign of his love and concern.

They were only together for a short time before Mandela's

Nelson Mandela poses with his new bride Winnie Madikizela in June 1958, in what was then Ponderland, South Africa. GAMMA-RAPHO VIA GETTY IMAGES

political work took him from her, first into the underground and then to prison, where she visited him often. Together they had two girls, who had an especially hard upbringing once Winnie herself became deeply politicized. Winnie was harassed, jailed, beaten, and banished by the government. At one point she was kept in solitary confinement and tortured. Her children were often left alone.

In Nelson's absence, Winnie became the voice of the ANC inside South Africa, upholding the Mandela name, and inspiring women in South Africa and around the world. She became a well-known leader in her own right, one who galvanized youth activism, including the Soweto Uprising when, she says, the martyr of that movement, the slain Hector Pieterson, was actually living at her house. Later, decisions and associations she made as a self-styled "Mother of the Nation" generated controversy, trials, and scandal.

The movie does not sanitize her experience, according to Nicholson: "That story, the love story, which is a very complex story, is basically a tragedy. And as the demands of the struggle are imposed upon him, it essentially destroys the heart of his life: his love for Winnie.

It was to Winnie that Mandela wrote many love letters during his long years in prison. It was she alone that he pined for and longed to see. It was also she who, as he aged, in her loneliness, began to have affairs and abandoned him, leading to a painful separation and divorce.

Added Nicholson, "Winnie was not in prison—I mean, she was in and out of prison. But Winnie was the one who was effectively being tortured. Winnie was put through enormous torments,

both physically—sleep deprivation and lengthy interrogation—
and psychologically. She was being taken away from her children
exactly when they were expecting to meet her so they would not
know what was happening to her. And all of this turned her into
somebody who was filled with anger and hatred.

"And why wouldn't it? I mean, if I had been put through that I
would be filled with anger and hatred, too. And it convinced her
that the only way forward was all-out war. And she was coming
to this conclusion even as Mandela in prison was reaching the
opposite conclusion. . . . You couldn't dream up as powerful, dramatic a conflict as that."

ARCHBISHOP Desmond Tutu told me about a dinner he and his
wife shared with the two Mandelas, who the world saw as an
almost magic couple.

"Soon after he was released, [Archbishop Tutu's wife] Leah
and I invited he and Winnie to come and have a Xhosa meal. . . .
And when they arrived it was quite, I mean you could see he
really was smitten. You have seen a puppy that loves its master?
He was very much like that. If she got up, his eyes were just for
her. He really loved her very deeply. Very, very deeply.

"And it's one of the deepest pains that he experienced, that
their relationship should have gone haywire as it did. And so
what you're saying about the depth of his suffering, that it was
not just a notion of a thing, it was something very personal. Not
to be able to touch his children, always to be speaking to them
with a glass partition separating them, was more than we can
imagine. I mean, the anguish of it. . . . You saw the cost.

"We spoke after he decided he was going to leave Soweto to

go and live in town. We had a very deep discussion . . . where a man shares things that he wouldn't normally want to share with another man, about what was happening in his own home, and why he had decided he had to leave. And I realized that the extent of his suffering did not end on Robben Island. It continued. And it is one of the most wonderful things that he should have found Graça."

GRAÇA MACHEL, Mandela's third wife, had been married to the Mozambican freedom fighter–turned-president Samora Machel, who was killed in a suspicious plane crash. She had been minister of education in her country and was respected worldwide as a child advocate, for the depth of her compassion, for her eloquence, for her sophistication. Like Mandela, she had suffered the loss of someone who had been both her great love and her political comrade.

Mandela announced at his eightieth birthday party that he and Machel had been married the day before, on his eightieth birthday. When a man known for keeping all emotions in check kissed Machel in front of everyone, it thrilled those present.

But even as he abandoned bachelorhood once more, he was still known for his flirtatiousness around women. Observed the film's researcher Gail Behrmann, "Women love him and he loves women. After he came out of prison, if you were doing an interview with him, he would always single out the woman in the group."

The movie's casting director Moonyeen Lee told us, "I've only met Mandela three times. Every time I've met him, as old as I am, he flirted with me. And it's a natural thing that he's got, and he's so charming.

Cheryl Carolus, a grassroots activist turned ANC official and now a top businesswoman, laughed about his flirtatiousness, telling me, "Madiba, Nelson Mandela, is an outrageous flirt. Totally outrageous flirt! But very chivalrous . . . very charming. I don't deal with people who I feel are sexist or trying to hit on me. And I think he can get away with it any time because he's so charming about it."

Mandela is conscious of his behavior and is even self-critical about it now, according to the South African historian Verne Harris who is the director of Research and Archive at Madiba's own Centre of Memory in Johannesburg: "He's not a saint. I think for me one of his most endearing attributes is precisely his determination to keep learning as a human being, to keep liberating himself even late in his life, so in terms of his relations with and attitudes to women, he was a product of his time and of his context. By his own admission, when he went to Robben Island he was a male chauvinist, and it took long years of study and of reading and working for his own prejudices to reach the point that it's reached now."

I asked Verne if Madiba acknowledges flaws that could undermine his image.

After a thoughtful pause, Verne told me what Mandela told him: "'I'm an ordinary human being.' And then he told us something that I think is of crucial importance institutionally in setting up the Centre of Memory. He said to us, 'You don't have to protect me.' In other words, we don't have to be gatekeepers. He's given us a mandate to go into those difficult spaces, the mistakes he's made and the flaws that he's carried as an individual."

Even as Mandela reached out for the affection of women, he was also very ethical in his attitude toward using exposés of sexual relations against his enemies. In his *Memoirs*, Ahmed Kathrada recounted an incident that showed an almost Victorian side to Mandela's sensibility. A *Kirkus* review of Kathy's book noted:

> In one memorable scene, Kathrada described placing an inebriated political enemy in a compromising situation involving a prostitute. However, once the pictures were snapped and the evidence gathered, he brought them to Mandela who, rather than encouraging their publication, helped Kathrada weigh the moral cost of destroying a man's career simply for disagreeing with his politics. After much reflection, Kathrada destroyed the incriminating photos, sparing the man his much-deserved shame while revealing an instance of rare civility when none was ever offered to him.

What are Mandela's regrets? According to journalist Richard Stengel, who worked with him on *Long Walk to Freedom*, he is filled with them, especially about his family and his marriages. Stengel told an interviewer for American public television about a bigger question he wrestles with: "He has certain regrets even about whether it was all worthwhile."

MILITANT

WHEN HE walked out of prison after twenty-seven-and-a-half years, Nelson Mandela initially reinforced his public image as a militant revolutionary: Walking hand in hand with then wife Winnie through the gates at Victor Verster Prison, he came face to face with hundreds of people and scores of cameras—a media army had amassed to cover his historic release, alongside crowds of T-shirt–wearing and toyi-toying supporters. Winnie took the lead and threw her fist in the air. Mandela's fist quickly followed. The image was frozen in time. And even though the prison now has a new name, it also features a statue out front with the world's most famous political prisoner, fist in the air—a remarkable image of militancy for the world to see.*

Later, as he became a negotiator and then president, that militant image softened, wrote David Africa, an independent security analyst, for Aljazeera:

> This image of Mandela is one that has been aggressively cultivated since his elevation from prisoner to president with the first democratic election in 1994, and is a curious part of a political project with the twin objectives of moderating

---

* A replica of that statue and its militant pose also now graces South Africa's embassy in Washington, DC, across the street from a more formal statue of Winston Churchill, whose memoirs Mandela read while in prison.

one of the primary symbols of the South African liberation struggle on the one hand, and appropriating this "new Mandela" for a moderate or even conservative political project.

The Mandela we know has always been a militant, from his days as a fiery youth leader in the 1940s, through leading the . . . Defiance Campaign against the apartheid government in 1952 and then as the first commander of that organization's armed wing when it turned to violent resistance in 1961.

It was Mandela, too, who had crafted what was called the "M Plan" (for Mandela), to prepare contingencies for the movement being forced underground. Ronnie Kasrils, who became a commander in the MK armed struggle, and later an intelligence minister, worked alongside Mandela when he was underground. He recalled:

"He was a man of defiance. He led the masses in militant active struggle, and he led us in armed struggle. This is conveniently forgotten under the olive branch of Mandela the Saint. If one has to understand him in total, you've got to look back to the man who with his colleagues, with his contemporaries, created this ANC, led our people through chapters of struggle, and then at a crucial point when nonviolent struggle became an impossible way to change the system, putting his head together with others, including with young people and the rank and file, was saying, 'We've got to find another way, and now we need to rise up with weapons.'"

Or, as Mandela himself remembered: "I had no epiphany, no singular revelation, no moment of truth. But a steady accumulation of a thousand slights, a thousand indignities, and a thousand unremembered moments produced in me an anger, a rebelliousness, a desire to fight the system that imprisoned my people."

Mandela's days as the commander in chief of Umkhonto stirred many followers. Former MK guerrilla "Tokyo" Sexwale told me that after he was captured, he looked forward to being sent to Robben Island, because this meant he was going to meet his leader, Mandela.

When I visited Thabo Mbeki at home, I was startled at first by the wall photo on prominent display, of a bearded and much younger Mandela together with his ANC comrades, taken when he visited them while they were guests of Algerian revolutionaries based in Morocco. There is a great deal of nostalgia about this side of Mandela, the man of peace who transformed himself into a military leader.

Why should it even matter what he is called? I asked myself. He was a militant when militancy was what was needed, and then more of a moderate when he began speaking out for reconciliation.

Biographer Anthony Sampson recalled, in a US public television interview, what Mandela was like during his period of maximum militancy:

> I first consciously got to know him really in the Defiance Campaign, which was his first major protest organization, when he was the chief volunteer. That's when he really emerged for the first time as being a serious political leader. He was clearly a formidable one; but to me, anyway, he was quite distant. He was not easy to communicate with in the way that Sisulu absolutely was.

Partly, as he says now, he was defensive, particularly amongst white people, when they were not directly part of the political scene. And I wasn't part of the ANC or the Communist Party. At the same time, he did have that aloofness towards other people, too, even to people like Ruth First, who was a great, loyal party member, who found him quite arrogant, though she would become very close to Mandela in many ways.

Sampson was asked, "Would you say that anger, that sense of humiliation, would account for why he was interested in pursuing the political life?"

"The aggression, at that time, was considerable, yes. The aggression pressed him into politics. Of course, the city life made him feel that he was part of a much larger society, who were suffering in a way that he hadn't properly comprehended, or hadn't felt before he came to Johannesburg. So it was a combination of the personal humiliations, which were almost visible every day, together with the awareness of being part of this bigger scene."

On a visit to Stanford University, Sampson once told an interviewer:

"Mandela's story is so like a fairy tale in that it's very easy to become sentimental about it," he said. "He is the ultimate hero, imprisoned by the wicked witch in a dungeon, who is magically released and turns out to be a prince. It's always dangerous to get sentimental about politics, particularly in Africa. When Mandela asked me to write his biography in 1996, he particularly insisted that he wanted to be regarded as an ordinary man and portrayed in his vices as well as his virtues."

ANOTHER MANDELA scholar and close observer, Tom Lodge, credited his upbringing, including his exposure to the Thembu aristocracy and Anglophile education for grooming his leadership skills. "Mandela's self-conscious charisma, graceful manners, and a deeply ingrained sense of political tolerance proved key to his effectiveness as a leader," according to Lodge.

At the same time, his close friendships often encouraged a form of "populist cronyism" that the historian Anthony Butler has attributed to a lack of accountability and an indifference toward corruption. Another biographer, Martin Meredith, has stressed the changes that South Africa went through since Mandela's release from prison, writing in *Mandela: A Biography*:

"The truth is that Mandela mellowed in prison, and realized the limits of protest. His 'struggle credentials' were secure. He then had a new role to play."

It became clear to him that the government was under intense political and economic pressure and could not maintain the status quo forever.

BY THE MID-1980s, the ANC's four-pronged strategy—of encouraging unrest in the townships, seeking economic sanctions and diplomatic isolation, mobilizing antiapartheid activism worldwide, and mounting an armed struggle—was having an impact.

Soon, activists in exile began to sense the beginning of the end. ANC leader Thabo Mbeki was tasked in Lusaka, by Oliver Tambo, to explore an informal track of dialogue and negotiations with Afrikaner leaders and South African businesses.

The ANC's leadership nexus had shifted away from Robben Island. The island prison was no longer the epicenter of resistance.

Thabo Mbeki explained to me: "At some point it became clear to some of us that the possibility existed for a negotiated resolution of the South African question [to complement Mandela's negotiations inside]. But it meant that we had to do a number of things, one of which was to try and move as much of the white population in South Africa as possible away from a fear of the ANC, and, an allegiance to the apartheid system and the apartheid regime. This required a lot of interaction with the sector of our population in politics, in business, in the church, the media, everywhere—so that they would change their attitude toward the ANC, which would result in them distancing themselves from the regime. . . . We had to engage in a similar sort of process internationally."

He said that the Afrikaner government, under pressure from banking sanctions and intensified international condemnation, recognized it could no longer just demonize and avoid the ANC.

Added Mbeki: "As far as the National Party was concerned, indeed, I think, they were now quite set that first of all they had to talk to the ANC. They couldn't avoid that. Then, secondly, that in the process of that interaction they would indeed convince us to adopt a particular position which would be consistent with what they thought should happen, and they did believe that—"

I interjected, suggesting what I imagine he may have been told, "'Thabo, be reasonable with us. Be reasonable. This can't be done overnight.' Was that the sort of tone?"

"No, it was not so much that as them insisting that we understand how South Africa is constituted. In reality, what they kept presenting was the same notion of apartheid, separate development, South Africa as a community of nationalities, with distinct cultures and all of that. And therefore the new political system you had to construct had to take into account that kind of reality. That was basically the point they were trying to put across, so that in the end, it doesn't matter what form it would take, in the end what you would have is a modified system of apartheid. With our permission and our support!"

There were displays of militancy in this period—uprisings in the townships and a sharp police response. It was a time of massive protests and mass movements. It became clear that if there was to be progress toward majority rule through a peaceful process, there would have to be negotiations. That was the next step. The time was now.

Mandela has come a long way, his biographer Sampson has said. The Mandela he first met "could be somewhat vain and rash," and was too enthralled with "half-baked, Marxist ideas." Mandela struck Sampson as a showman, but one who was constantly growing and changing.

In 1964, Madiba asked Sampson to look over a draft of his opening statement for the Rivonia Trial, as Sampson would tell John Sanford at Stanford University:

"So I had the chance to see this speech, in a draft, which revealed the extent of his development. What would become two of his most distinguishing traits, dignity and poise, were readily apparent."

"So, as a situation that had been in stasis for so long began quickly to change, so did the ANC's 'militant' leader?" I asked Sahm Venter of the Mandela Centre of Memory. His answer: "Not as much as you would think."

"What I have learned studying all this material," Venter elaborated, "is that he did not change at all. In fact, the world changed. He went in with a set of beliefs and a set of standards—say, for example, the one he expressed in 1961 at the All In Africa Conference. They called for a convention on a nonracial democracy, and promised if not there would be a strike. He was ignored, went into jail, [and] came out calling for basically the same thing. He didn't compromise his principles at all. All he did was get older."

NEGOTIATOR

THERE IS a comic book about Nelson Mandela called *The Negotiator*, an indication that his Centre of Memory wants the public, especially young people, to value the art of negotiation as a weapon of change. A song that is sung in schools also teaches this "N" word:

> He set out to change and transform,
> the whole country one mind at a time.
> Joined the African National Congress,
> ANC, what's that? Y'all gonna have to wait and see.
> At first he tried to talk and **negotiate**,
> Deal with the government, start bargaining.
> But his talks were met with silence,
> So as a last resort he turned to violence.
> But he was prosecuted and put on trial,
> The judge said, "You're going to go to jail for a while."

Nelson Mandela was a fighter for freedom, but also a lawyer who recognized that his movement needed to negotiate with its enemies. There's an old saying that to achieve progress, you can't just negotiate with your friends. Sometimes, you need to break the ice first before enemies will sit down with their adversaries, especially those who have been trying to kill each other. You have to overcome distrust, cultivate trust, and find a way to agree on an agenda.

And ultimately, you need to have the support of your comrades, and in a larger sense, of your constituency, the people, as Mandela emphatically believed, though he pointedly started talking first with the government without his movement's okay. But to finish those negotiations, as he said repeatedly, the ANC had to negotiate collectively, as a team.

And that's exactly what they went on and did, with many lawyers including Joe Slovo playing a major role. When he had practiced law, Mandela was known as a fierce cross-examiner and questioner. Anthony Sampson quoted a Botswanan freedom fighter, Michael Dingake, about what it was like to argue with Madiba in the university-like classes they offered on Robben Island: "In arguments with someone with insubstantial facts, Nelson could be vicious, adopting a modified Socratic method. Very few people like to be cross-examined and exposed in their vagueness and ignorance. Going against Nelson was the worst. He took no prisoners." (In a prison!)

Cyril Ramaphosa, the labor leader turned businessman, was the chief negotiator of the ANC's first negotiating team. He described the process that ultimately led to agreements: "Coming from two completely different backgrounds, two completely different histories, and representing organizations that have completely different strategic objectives, we found that . . . we could share the common vision . . . to resolve the apartheid problem and to introduce democracy in our country. . . . There were times during the negotiations when . . . we didn't see eye to eye on a number of issues. And we always said there is no problem without a solution. After that we found trust developing on an ongoing basis."

Roelf Meyer, former minister of constitutional affairs and chief government negotiator—and Ramaphosa's main adversary—credited the personal relationships that developed between the two sides as critical. "The aspect of personal relationship was one of the most important parts of the process."

There is a famous story of Meyer and Ramaphosa going fishing together. When a fishing hook goes into Ramaphosa's thumb, the other pulls it out. The small moment of kindness cements a friendship, and becomes a metaphor for the unity that both sides want to achieve—even if each on their own terms.

Cheryl Carolus, a member of the ANC's first group of negotiators, credited the ANC activists for winning the confidence of their adversaries: "That's what the Nationalist Party could not get over. Not only were they very clever people, these ANC leaders, but they were actually incredibly human, caring people. People did worry when one of them, of the National Party, had terrible flu. They would worry about the person, ask if they were okay, if they felt well enough to continue, ask, did they have some medication? Is there a doctor in the house? . . ."

Ramaphosa summed up the spirit of those times: "You could say that South Africa is a nation of negotiators. The beauty of the negotiation process that brought about the end of apartheid is that it has really caught fire in this country."

Journalist Allister Sparks told me, "I don't know of another situation which has gone through the kind of negotiated revolution we've undergone. . . . this country is a model for global politics and that is why it should be studied more seriously than . . . simply [as] a battle between black and white."

NELSON MANDELA symbolized and led the process. He gave it a moral authority even when violence in the country and bad faith among the parties threatened to derail it. As a politician, Mandela brought a can-do spirit, wrangling with the different opposing parties—and wrestling with factions in the shifting alliances within his own party—inviting all to take part in the process and give it a chance.

Later, after he became president of South Africa, Mandela was often called upon to use his negotiating skills on domestic and international issues. He tried but failed to negotiate a political settlement in the Democratic Republic of the Congo, but was more successful in Burundi. He became part of a group of ex-presidents and world leaders called "The Elders," whose influence was used to help in solving other global problems. His commitment to collective decision-making, by definition, kept him in a negotiating mode as he wrestled with what would be South Africa's future moving forward.

IN THE negotiations, the ANC's main goal was to end apartheid and forge a multiracial democracy on a one man–one vote basis. Africa's first independent leader, Kwame Nkrumah of Ghana, had advised his followers, "Seek Ye First the Political Kingdom," a perspective shared by many ANC stalwarts. Winning political power, they believed, would allow them to transform the country.

The problem with that view was that South Africa was not just ruled by an all-white political party, but also by an economic system controlled by an oligarchy of big businesses—known locally as the Mineral Energy Complex (MEC). Moreover, in the age of globalization, when financial markets and big banks based on

Wall Street or in London have global leverage and control over what emerging countries can and cannot do, international business forces also wielded enormous power and control.

The ANC wanted to transform the country, not just take it over. They wanted to end poverty and share the country's resources. Running for office in 1994, when free elections were finally held, their slogan was "A Better Life for All."

But to achieve that goal, there had to be economic negotiations as well as political ones, as former Congress of South African Trade Unions (COSATU) leader Jay Naidoo knew all too well. Mandela appointed Naidoo to his cabinet to run the Reconstruction and Development Program (RDP), the ANC's first attempt to use power for economic ends. The RDP was resisted by, and under pressure from, the business sector from day one.

Naidoo explained the context to me: "The Berlin Wall had just collapsed. The US was triumphant in the fight and war against Communism. And we had this phase of triumphant capitalism, that the market and capital were gonna deliver the millions and billions of people in the world from their poverty. So, suddenly, you had a phase in which you started to, in a sense, reduce the prominence of very important parts of our struggle—which was around economic equality, social solidarity, human dignity—and start[ed] to celebrate a model that more profiled individualism, and profiled the idea that, 'If you fail, it's your own fault.'"

Naidoo and others in the ANC wanted to negotiate those issues but failed to win the full support of the ANC and Mandela himself, who, by then, was being cultivated and lobbied personally by influential top business leaders in South Africa and overseas, all with advice and warnings about the danger of government intervention in the economy. They were meeting with him, and promising that the market could create the jobs the country needed.

Added Naidoo: "We wanted to have a negotiation around the structural problems that our economy faced. How are you going to sustainably address issues of structural unemployment in the country, when there was a very low education level for the majority of black people? And how are you going to promote jobs, and enterprises that create jobs? So we were defeated in that agenda."

Years later, in the annual Nelson Mandela lecture delivered on Madiba's birthday, his successor and former deputy president Thabo Mbeki warned against building the "New South Africa" around the dictates of the market:

"I believe that for us to ensure that things do not fall apart, we must, in the first instance, never allow that the market should be the principal determinant of the nature of our society.

"We should firmly oppose the 'market fundamentalism' which George Soros has denounced as the force that has led society to lose its anchor. Instead, we must place at the center of our daily activities the pursuit of the goals of social cohesion and human solidarity."

Mbeki's words would be too late, however, because by the time he said them, South Africa had already rebuilt itself around the market, partly at his urging. Here's how Professor Patrick Bond of the University of KwaZulu-Natal explained what really happened in that period, in his study, *Elite Transition*:

> The unbanning of South Africa's liberation organizations and the release of Nelson Mandela in February 1990

provided a moment of uncertainty—of perhaps five or six years' duration—when, it seemed to most observers, nearly any kind of political-economic future was possible. The existence of fluidity within and around the ANC heightened the country's already intense ideological and factional struggles. There was little doubt that an overhaul of the country's notoriously inefficient, skewed and stagnant economy was in store, but the forces that would set the parameters during the crucial first half of the decade were by no means evident.

It was an auspicious time, for while still serving his last month in prison, Mandela insisted that the Freedom Charter demands for "the nationalization of mines, banks and monopoly industries is the policy of the ANC and a change or modification of our views in this regard is inconceivable."

Mandela's statement was not dismissed as idle chatter on Diagonal Street. As *Business Day* glumly put it the next day, the statement "will set back the hopes of those moving towards acceptance of majority rule in the belief that free enterprise and individual property rights would still be possible."

But such hopes—and extensive "scenario planning" efforts to draw ANC and some trade union leaders up the oft-cited "learning curve" (which quickly turned out instead to be a steep forgetting curve for former shop floor or street-smart activists)—were soon to be richly rewarded. . . . Indeed, not only were free enterprise and property rights enshrined in every major economic policy

statement and the Constitution itself, full-blown neoliberal *compradorism* became the dominant (if not universal)
phenomenon within the ANC policy-making elite.

Six months before the 1994 elections, when South Africa was
being governed jointly by the ANC and the National Party under
a Transitional Executive Council (TEC), there were secret negotiations about the economic future. According to the Afrikaner
economist and historian Sampie Terreblanche of Stellenbosch
University—who at one point was an economist for the all-white
government and had also been a member of the Broederbond,
the secret Afrikaner society that ran apartheid behind the
scenes—"Mr. Mandela was released on the eleventh of February, 1990. I was informed that Mr. Mandela has a weekly lunch
or dinner appointment with Harry Oppenheimer, the CEO, the
big boss of Anglo-American, the biggest gold mine and diamond
industry company in the world.

"They met regularly from '90 to '91. Then there were regular
meetings at Little Brenthurst—it is the estate, a remarkable
estate, in the middle of Jo'burg—when more people from
the business world joined. Then Little Brenthurst was not big
enough. And you must see that there were two sets of negotiations in the early years of the 1990s.

"The negotiations on South Africa's future political system,
the so-called CODESA negotiations, were public. But these other
negotiations were secret and took place during the night in the
SA Development Bank between Jo'burg and Pretoria. . . . At the
secret negotiations, the Mineral Energy Complex, the MEC,
played the dominant role."

Mandela gives his first speech as a freed man in Cape Town, February 11, 1990. Labor leader Cyril Ramaphosa holds the microphone. Winnie is behind him. ANC leader Walter Sisulu is at his right. CHRIS LEDOCHOWSKI/SOUTH PHOTOGRAPHS/AFRICA MEDIA ONLINE

It sounded to me more like a conspiracy than a negotiation.

"When they reached agreement, more or less, they decided that South Africa needed a loan of $850 million to solve some of our foreign exchange problems. The international monetary fund was prepared to give us the money on one condition: that all sixteen members—half representing the ANC, half representing the government—had to sign a document. If one reads that document carefully, one sees that it is nothing but the Washington Consensus. South Africa had to commit itself to fiscal austerity, to liberalization, to privatization, to all these things. So some people called it a sell-out."

"A sell-out? That sounds very strong."

"Call it a sell-out, an elite compromise, or the elite conspiracy, call it what you like, it happened six months before the general election of 1994. In sum, the economic philosophy that was favored by the US in Washington, in London, at the big banks, and the values behind it, were imposed on the negotiating parties. They said, 'We'll give you the money but you have to agree to our terms.'"

IN THEIR 2012 book, *Who Rules South Africa?*, journalists Martin Plaut and Paul Holden wrote that the ANC had little grasp on how to transform the economy. International investors opposed nationalization on principle. Nationalization was viewed as "socialistic" at a time that the socialist countries were collapsing. When Mandela visited the World Economic Forum in 1991 and again a year later, he was advised—not just by capitalists but by leaders of socialist countries like Vietnam as well, to promote a mixed economy. His original speech was promptly modified to appease that sentiment.

I asked historian Verne Harris of the Mandela Centre of Memory about this. I expected he would dismiss it. He didn't. Here's part of our exchange:

"I think there's an element of truth in that. . . . I think that under Madiba's leadership the ANC embraced a neoliberal agenda with unseemly haste and we're paying a terrible price for that now. . . . We're only beginning to understand the nature of this phenomenon. From the late 1980s, a huge seduction was underway, of the liberation movement by capital and it's playing out in all kinds of destructive ways now, from arms deals to corruption. We're having it at all levels of our society."

In his biography of Mandela, Anthony Sampson acknowledged, "Mandela had no experience in economics, but he accepted the imperatives of the global marketplace." In furtherance of this market logic, he appointed Derek Keys, de Klerk's pro-market finance minister as his own, and then, when he stepped down, replaced him with Chris Liebenberg, a banker. He kept Chris Stals, a conservative former member of the Broederbond, on the Reserve Bank. In essence, he said, "the old guard was running what to all the world looked like a new show."

Ronnie Kasrils, the MK commander turned government minister, looked back on this history and wondered whether compromises made then sealed the country's fate, in effect blocking deeper social change. Twenty years later, in a new 2013 introduction to his autobiography, *Armed and Dangerous*, Kasrils wrote:

What I call our Faustian moment came when we took an IMF loan on the eve of our first democratic election. That

loan, with strings attached that precluded a radical economic agenda, was considered a necessary evil, as were
concessions to keep negotiations on track and take delivery of the promised land for our people. Doubt had come
to reign supreme: we believed, wrongly, there was no
other option, that we had to be cautious, since by 1991
our once powerful ally, the Soviet Union, bankrupted by
the arms race, had collapsed. Inexcusably, we had lost
faith in the ability of our own revolutionary masses to
overcome all obstacles. Whatever the threats to isolate a
radicalizing South Africa, the world could not have done
without our vast reserves of minerals.

To lose our nerve was not necessary or inevitable. The
ANC leadership needed to remain determined, united
and free of corruption—and, above all, to hold on to its
revolutionary will. Instead, we chickened out. The ANC
leadership needed to remain true to its commitment of
serving the people. This would have given it the hege-
mony it required not only over the entrenched capitalist
class but over emergent elitists, many of whom would
seek wealth through black economic empowerment, corrupt practices and selling political influence.

Kasrils had hoped the West would commit to a "new Marshall
Plan,"—like the one that led to the reconstruction of Europe
after World War II—to rebuild South Africa's apartheid-rav-
aged economy, but the West did not respond. Instead, Western
financial agencies counseled more privatization and fewer jobs
in the face of dramatic unemployment. South Africa's needs and

the hopes of its people were not persuasive to a self-interested US-dominated economic order, he said.

Later, in a conversation with Richard Stengel for his last book, *Conversations with Myself*, Mandela revealed that American businessmen put a lot of pressure on the ANC to drop its initial commitment to nationalization. Mandela recounted meeting many leaders at the World Economic Forum who advised against it and he admits, "We had to remove the fear of business that . . . their assets will be nationalized."

Jay Naidoo has agreed that many of South Africa's current problems go back to what was resolved or not resolved in the negotiations, but he doesn't blame Nelson Mandela:

"These were our decisions. The decision to replace the RDP with a macroeconomic program that just focused on the financial industries was our decision. No one made it for us. We have to hold ourselves accountable for that. And that document was drafted in secret. Not even the ANC office bearer saw it. Not even the national executive committee of the ANC saw it. We saw it on the day it was published. So there was a conspiracy in our own ranks which obviously had interacted with very powerful economic forces in the country, and felt that the RDP was too radical."

Naidoo's conclusion is hard to argue with: "We have created a Molotov cocktail in this country. And all that we see today, the violence that we see, the anger that we see, is a consequence of those decisions that we made then. I don't hold Mandela responsible for it. Sometimes I hold myself responsible. It's my generation that has failed the country."

But these problems were not caused simply by personal failures. South Africa was never in the driver's seat when it came to its economy. It was subject to decisions about trade and investment made elsewhere. Also, the ANC government never controlled the economic levers that were dominated domestically by a small number of banks and companies that may have praised Nelson Mandela as a leader, but didn't necessarily listen to him in terms of his government's priorities.

In interviews with key decision makers in the ANC and in the ANC-led government that took place over a period of years, scholar Padraig O'Malley kept asking local leaders about these issues. Often the responses were overly optimistic or indicated a lack of knowledge about who was calling the shots in economic terms.

Here is an interview from May 17, 1996, between O'Malley and Pallo Jordan:

PADRAIG: Unemployment. Stuck. No improvement being made at all. At the same time we pick up *Business Day* every other day and you see that corporate profits are soaring. Where are the corporate profits going? Are they being ploughed back into technology that eliminates jobs or are they being distributed to shareholders or are they being siphoned off into other investments that are essentially non-productive in terms of creating jobs?

PALLO: What I think we're stuck with is limited growth, but growth without job creation. And perhaps we need much more rapid growth, to increase the growth rate to something like 6% to make that sort of impact. But of course one of the problems, I think, is that new technologies tend to be more capital- than labor-intensive. One is going to have to look much more at your public works programs for the immediate, for your job creation programs, and one is also going to have to look to your small- and medium-size enterprises and encouraging those as job creators. They tend to be much more effective job creators than your large corporations. Perhaps not sufficient attention has been paid to encouraging that sector because I think you will note also that even with your black economic empowerment programs lots of those are targeting the big corporate giants rather than seeing the emergence of small- and medium-size enterprises.

And around and around the discourse went but, perhaps because of the government's pro-market neoliberal direction, as well as pressure from elites and fear of alienating local and global business, reforming the economy wasn't given the attention it deserved. Politicians tended to rule over politics, while big business, in South Africa like elsewhere in the world, have mostly demanded a free hand to run the economy.

IN 2013, I asked Thabo Mbeki for his perspective on what went wrong. He was Mandela's deputy president before serving as president for nine years himself. His take: "I think that the fundamental problems of South Africa have remained unchanged since that transition in 1994. The fundamental problems of poverty, of inequality. And therefore when people talk about national reconciliation, national cohesion and all that, you have to address these fundamental questions. What is it that needs to be done in order to eradicate poverty? What is it that needs to be done to bridge these enormous gaps in terms of wealth, of income of opportunity, and so on, between black and white, men and women, and all that. That's what South Africa must address. And, indeed, that brings us back then to the question that you were raising.

"One of the problems, one of the challenges that we have never been able to solve in all of these years since our liberation, is the attitude of white capital. Even today, I promise you as we're talking now, there are large volumes of investable money that South African companies are holding in cash, and not investing in the economy. And this has been the situation ever since '94, driven by a fear that, 'It's inevitable that there will be a crisis. And because there will be a crisis, inevitably, I must hold as much of my assets in liquid form as possible, so that if I have to run, I can't upend the factory because I can't move it, but at least the money I can run away with.' It's a persistent problem."

ONWARD

IN HIS sunset years, as he grows older and frailer, Mandela's legacy is being solidified and debated, as is natural. In South Africa, his iconic status has already assured his legacy as the Father of the Nation, a virtual demigod. When he was in the hospital for medical tests and treatments, the current president, Jacob Zuma, went so far as to issue a statement begging the media to allow Mandela the dignity and respect he is entitled to—both as a private citizen, and as the country's founding democratic president and a national hero, whose every breath has become an international news story.

The Christian Science Monitor described how "the great regard that South Africans hold for their nonagenarian former president is wrapped up in the extraordinary saga of Mandela's role in fighting for full democratic rights, and later, for holding South Africa together during one of the most difficult transitions in its history."

Sarah Nuttall, the director of the Wits Institute for Social and Economic Research, saw all this in more personal terms for Mandela in an April 2013 article in the *Mail & Guardian*:

> A complex dialectics of presence and absence, disappearance and reappearance have been a hallmark of Mandela's life, from the time he went underground in 1961 to his re-emergence to freedom in 1990. Because of this, Mandela's actual death will be anything but a sudden death.

Nor will his death open on to total absence—his life having been lived as a long oscillation between encounter,
distance and separation, solitude and conviviality, the
life of the day and the life of the night.

He has experienced the deaths of members of his family and
political comrades that hurt him deeply, and at one point in his
life he faced his own death when he was a defendant in the Rivonia Trial for sabotage.

Wrote Nuttall:

> One of the trialists' lawyers, Joel Joffe, wrote: "On our
> way home we stopped at the jail to talk to the accused.
> They were calm, living now in the shadow of death. The
> strain and tension was becoming almost unbearable, yet
> the only matter they wanted to discuss was how they
> should behave in court if the death sentence was passed."
>
> Informed that the judge would ask him whether
> he had any reason to advance why the death sentence
> should not be passed, Mandela responded that he was
> "prepared to die for his beliefs, and knew that his death
> would be an inspiration to his people in their strug-
> gle." There is "no easy walk to freedom. We have to pass
> through the shadow of death again and again before we
> reach the mountaintops of our desires."

Even as activists and athletes and entertainers honor him
by responding to his call for engagement on his birthday, July
18, now celebrated as Mandela Day, a time for community ser-

vice, journalists in the obituary departments of the world's news networks are quietly, even secretly, combing their archives for footage and tributes that will air when he moves onto the next world. They are getting ready and seem to think it will happen sooner rather than later.

Mandela's death may receive more visibility than the great achievements of his long life.

The question is: Which Mandela will be memorialized? Will it be the leader who built a movement and a military organization to fight injustice? Or a man of inspiration with a great smile whom we admire because of the long years he suffered behind bars?

Having spent many years as a network producer, I know that the television news industry's instinct is to "humanize" the departed by focusing on their symbolic importance. The funerals of Ronald Reagan and Margaret Thatcher received days of reverential, noncritical print and television coverage.

This approach also involves softening, celebrating, and depoliticizing a completely political person who said famously, "The struggle is my life," in the interest of presenting someone who anybody could relate to, a big name to admire but not necessarily to learn from—someone, an image of a person, that's a bit blurrier than the real Nelson Mandela was.

We will have lost something immensely important if Mandela is memorialized as a cheery optimist. Sarah Nuttall described his retreats during moments of the most agonizing personal pain:

> Some of Mandela's most momentous engagements with death occurred while he was in prison. A pivotal space during his carceral years was the cell. It might not have

presented the strict appearance of a grave: measuring just more than 2m by 2m in size, its features were a mixture of a coffin and a catacomb. It was the actual instantiation of the harshness and grimness that surrounded him for decades. Whenever death struck, as we have seen, it is to his cell that he withdrew, or disappeared into. A physical space of confinement and solitude, the cell became a shroud, a space of mourning and confrontation with oneself and with the memory of the dead.

Significant during the Robben Island years are Mandela's dreams, almost always ghostly narratives. . . . Mandela wrote to Winnie: "Sometimes I feel like one who is on the sidelines . . . who has missed life itself."

Mandela's achievements—and sometimes lack of them—once in office are not as well known as they should be, while the story of how South Africa ended apartheid is reduced in some quarters to the waving of his magic wand.

The accent on TV news is always on top-down change by the great and the good—not the bottom-up pressure by freedom fighters at the community level, who made the country ungovernable with help from armed fighters in exile, United Nations resolutions, economic and cultural sanctions, pressure by anti-apartheid militants the world over, and even the might of the Cuban army that defeated the South Africans in Angola.

These are not the parts of his history that corporate media like to project—for fear of what it might encourage. The corporations and foundations that fund Mandela's foundation prefer to treat him as a do-good icon that everyone loves, not an agitator who, for years, the establishment hated. They stress his moderate calls for racial recognition, not his militant demands for equality.

During the decades he spent in prison, the government did everything they could to turn him into a nonperson. He could not be quoted in South Africa, and his picture could not be shown. The South Africans not only incarcerated him in their most remote and brutal dungeon, but they ensured that he disappeared from public view. Despite the isolation, he was not forgotten, organizing the men around him into a unit of resistance, and politically educating younger captives in what was dubbed "Robben Island University." The emphasis was on self-education and self-improvement, the outlook forward-looking. As one former inmate on "the island" told me, "We became prisoners of hope."

Mandela did this by co-opting and befriending prison guards, by speaking their language and finding out about their families, gradually weakening their hostility and violence. He was always very strategic. He learned to contain his anger and not succumb to hatred to ensure survival. He was so successful that, at one point, one of the prison chiefs asked him, "Mr. Mandela, may I have my prison back?"

As he mounted a protracted personal battle, he went inside himself, often hiding his personal feelings and vulnerabilities. Once he understood that he had become a role model, he acted the part, almost like a performance artist. As the world discovered his courage, South Africa had to take him more seriously as well, after the regime was flooded with demands to release him, from people worldwide, in all walks of life. To his growing ranks of followers, every utterance suddenly seemed profound, even when they weren't.

He went on to make deals with apartheid leaders, to blast

his negotiating partner F. W. de Klerk and then embrace him. He helped organize the country's first democratic election and made sure all parties were welcome to participate, because he understood deeply how important it was that all constituencies be invested in the future of South Africa. He consciously built alliances across racial, political, and tribal lines. He compromised some of his own principles in the name of avoiding a bloody civil war or reviving the economy. He then stepped down after one term, a rarity in Africa. He recognized the scourge of AIDS early on when some of his colleagues wouldn't.

This was his genius. It is the story of his great passion and perseverance over long decades of setback after setback. This is the story behind Mandela's "long walk to freedom."

His love life, the problems with his wife and his children and grandchildren may pull at our heartstrings, but they are not as important as the epic battles he led and ultimately won against injustice and for freedom.

After his death, this fight for freedom that inspired the world deserves telling, but which story do you think the networks will tell? Will they present him as victim or victor, as a flawed person, as he sees himself—or as a saint cleaned up and repackaged for mass consumption? Will they give us the one-dimensional Hollywood picture of the soft and endearing gentle giant that turns him into a grandfatherly cuddly bear, or the real saga of a liberation leader whose movement won against the odds?

Most South Africans have already decided to revere him for the sum of his contributions. Reported the *Monitor*: "What more do we want from him?" Archbishop emeritus Desmond Tutu asked reporters. "We want him to remain forever."

PRESIDENT

I would say breaking apartheid was less difficult than the challenges we are facing now. So while we are apportioning blame
and so forth, we should not forget that progress has been made,
significant progress has been made, but not enough for us to
say we are satisfied. We are only eighteen years old.

—AHMED "KATHY" KATHRADA

NELSON MANDELA'S learning curve went into higher gear when
he was released from prison to find his own party riven by divi-
sions and fierce debates about the future.

The first office he held after leaving prison was deputy president of the African National Congress. When president Oliver
Tambo suffered a stroke, Mandela was unanimously named ANC
president. In the negotiations for national elections, Mandela
once again was the ANC's first choice to be the party's candidate.

He didn't want to run, and at first demurred. This little-known
fact has been noted by Richard Stengel among others. Mandela
offered instead to advise whoever was elected. His comrades
argued with him, citing his own arguments for the importance of
collective leadership, and he relented—but with an unexpected
condition—that, if elected, he would only remain in office for
one term. He refused to change his mind about that decision,

which would be hailed by many when he actually kept to it, when so many presidents, once elected, seem to want to rule for life.

No one in the ANC had ever imagined a modern electoral media event like the election of 1994. The ANC leadership thought change would be the result of a military overthrow like the ones engineered through liberation wars in neighboring Mozambique and Zimbabwe. But they knew they stood little chance of winning against a government that was a major military power, with nearly 10 percent of the gross domestic product devoted to military spending.

For years, South Africa's repressive pro-apartheid government was intransigent, unwilling to reform or negotiate with its critics. And then, to everyone's surprise, the political dynamics changed unexpectedly and rapidly. The hardline National Party leader, P. W. Botha, was forced from office by his own party. Confrontations erupted in township after township. International pressure came not just from activists but from governments and bankers.

The ANC negotiated for—and won—a free election. Nelson Mandela was elected president of the republic of South Africa in the first-ever multiracial democratic election the country had ever seen. He was seventy-four years old, announcing that he would serve only one five-year term, a rare declaration by an African leader.

BEFORE THE election, the movement had to meet the challenge of transforming from an underground-driven movement into an open and accountable political party. They had to build an electoral machine to compete in a process that was being assembled by an Independent Electoral Commission. Unknown to many at the time, the ANC did what other political parties do and hired outside consultants to advise on strategy and to shape the message, working with support from President Bill Clinton and the United States' Democratic Party. (The Nationalist Party had its own outside advisors drawn from the conservative UK-based Saatchi & Saatchi advertising agency that had served on Margaret Thatcher's campaign.)

Steven Seidman wrote about this for the Communication Management and Design program at Ithaca College:

> The Mandela campaign was advised by American political consultant Stan Greenberg, who had advised Bill Clinton during his presidential election in the United States two years earlier. Greenberg utilized focus groups heavily to determine the campaign's main theme—that the ANC was an "agent of change," not a "liberation movement." In addition, he advised Mandela to soften his image.
>
> This image management can be seen in the poster of Mandela surrounded by children of all races—the smiling, grandfatherly change-agent who would work to help all the people look forward to a brighter future for their children. Along with the image manipulation, however, came specific goals: "2.5 million new jobs and 1 million new housing units within five years."

Greenberg's firm, Greenberg Quinlan Rosner Research, was paid well for its work. Using groundbreaking survey research conducted throughout South Africa, Greenberg Quinlan Rosner helped the ANC focus its campaign on people's aspiration toward achieving "a better life for all."

As the Greenberg Quinlan Rosner Research website stated: "This future-oriented, inclusive, optimistic framework allowed the ANC to present its plans and policies and emerge as the party ready to govern and lead. Conscious of the new context they were operating in, the ANC focused not just on mobilizing voters, but persuading them as well."

With the exception of the *Weekly Mail* and the *New Nation*, South Africa's press was against Mandela's election, fearing continued ethnic strife, instead supporting the National Party or the Democratic Party. Mandela became fundraiser-in-chief for the ANC, touring North America, Europe, and Asia meeting wealthy donors, including former supporters of the apartheid regime.

South African journalist Rich Mkondo, then with Reuters, explained the ANC's popularity on public television in America: "We South Africans are still in some kind of liberation mode. I was speaking to a friend of mine yesterday about the very same question. And I said to him, 'Why don't you vote for the other party?' And he says to me, 'Look, when I was struggling in the '60s and I was targeted by the police, it was the ANC that supported me. No one else supported me. I don't have a job now. . . . But I'm happy with the ANC. I'm going to vote for them for the next four elections,' which means it will take about twenty years for him to change his life."

I covered the election campaign for a film produced by Anant Singh, *Countdown for Freedom: The Ten Days That Changed South Africa*. We filmed most of the significant public events of that campaign and were also granted access by Mandela himself to shoot behind the scenes of what was being called a "liberation election." During the campaign I met Richard Stengel at a rally.

As we watched Mandela, surrounded by body guards he quipped, "He has become a prisoner again, still surrounded by guards."

It was obvious that the ANC, with its appeal to millions who had never voted before, would win. Officially, they received 63 percent of the vote, although there were rumors that the counting was stopped to insure that the opposition would have influence in Parliament in what was then labeled a "Government of National Unity." If the ANC received two-thirds of the vote, it would have been entitled to run the country unilaterally. The ANC feared that could lead to violence, so it was better to give the opposition a role. It was a political calculation that involved electoral manipulation.

The ANC's election advisors and consultants gave Mandela suggestions about how to be an effective candidate. He told me at the time, "They are our bosses and we listen to everything they say because they have the experience to guide us."

Winning the election was one thing, setting up an effective presidential office was another. Thabo Mbeki played a big role as the deputy president in organizing the bureaucracy and coordinating Mandela's efforts. Ahmed Kathrada, Madiba's prison mate, became a presidential counselor to take on special assignments.

Mandela understood that as president he now represented all South Africans. The career trajectory of Zelda La Grange—the young Afrikaner woman who started in the typing pool, became an assistant, then became his personal assistant in his post-presidential office all these years later—showed his willingness to include her Afrikaner culture in his administration.

La Grange said to me, "It might seem unlikely that he would

choose a white Afrikaans woman to work for him, but in 1994 I wasn't his private secretary. I didn't join as a secretary. I was a typist in his office. Then a certain working relationship was established, and then from that I grew into the position that I now have because he gave me the opportunity to do it.

"Eighteen years later I'm still connected to him as his personal assistant. I think it also has to do with the relationship that he had with Afrikaner people while he was in prison. He never detested Afrikaner people as people expected him to. He actually used his Afrikaner warders in prison to assist him in accomplishing his goals while he was incarcerated. So there has always been a role for Afrikaners in his life."

"Is there something in particular," I asked, "that enables him to work so well with people of other races and political persuasions?"

Zelda thought carefully about the question before responding. "I think one of his most underappreciated characteristics is really just the fact that he can deal with you for the person you are, the person that he faces, without paying attention to your skin color, your religion, your beliefs. He is good friends with people he opposed during apartheid after his release. So that doesn't influence how he deals with you today. Dealing with Afrikaner people, dealing with white people, he is able to take you as he finds you when he interacts with you."

"Weren't you scared? After all, you were brought up believing these people were terrorists?"

"I was very intimidated at first, being in an office that was run by the ANC. Although the party didn't run the government, there were close connections. The government was elected by the people, but the ANC organized how the government was run. So it was intimidating, coming from a very conservative background as I did.

"I was taught they were the terrorists, the enemies, they were out to kill us, that there was no point of a future behind the ANC coming into power. So it was extremely intimidating. I think maybe what was a very positive point at that stage was that I was very young and naïve. I didn't know too much about politics.

"So it was only about earning a salary, about doing the job, and, fortunately, I was brought up in a family where you do whatever it takes to make a success of your job. Whether you are a typist, whether you are vendor, whether you are a CEO, it isn't the position that matters, the position is nothing, it is hard work that matters. And that attitude that came from how I was raised was really what determined the rest of my life."

"Your first impression of Mandela?"

"The first thing I noticed was that he was quite tall. And then you noticed that he was old. He was an elderly statesman at that stage already. Then the feeling of guilt stepped in. My people, Afrikaner people, were responsible for apartheid and sent this man to jail. Yet the first thing he did was to reach out his hand to me. He greeted me. I was completely overcome with emotion. I started crying, and he spoke to me in Afrikaans, in my home language, and that was so touching."

La Grange described herself at that time as flustered, even fearful, worried about winning support from his whole team. But the team was sympathetic.

"The people that he appointed around him, the people in his press office, the people in his administration and the director general's office, were all people with political backgrounds who were politically savvy, and I took a lot of comfort in being able to share my fears with them in all honesty. They went to great lengths, I would say, to introduce me to politics with a soft landing. For one thing, they organized for me to go on a tour to Soweto. I had never been to Soweto before."

PRESIDENT MANDELA was popular but he did not, and probably could not, achieve all of his goals, said journalist and author David Goodman, who wrote a book about the challenges the ANC faced when it came into power.

"It's been very mixed results at this point. Certainly change can be measured in the number of water taps and electricity and telephones that have been brought to the poorer areas of South Africa. Certainly some of the worst hardships of poverty have been alleviated. [But] whether there can actually be opportunity created—that is, jobs, which really most black South Africans will tell you is their number one concern—that is what really remains as a challenge. In fact, South Africa has lost a half million jobs in the last five years."

FOR AHMED Kathrada, who followed Mandela from prison into the government, that's too simplistic an accounting. He said to me:

"To my mind, the most significant thing that has happened is not the material gains, but the material gains we have made in dignity. In the apartheid days, there was one sign, I have a replica of it, I will show you. It was a board that said, 'Non-Europeans, Traders and Dogs not allowed.' So Apartheid had reduced people who were not white to the level of animals. And you had these type of boards all over the country.

"So what we have won is our dignity, human dignity. All of us are equal. Racialism is a crime. So those are very significant things, huge things. No matter how wealthy or poor you are, living in the flats or in palaces, if you haven't got dignity, it is worthless. So we have equality. That we have achieved. But there is no dignity in poverty. There is no dignity in unemployment and hunger. So we can never be happy with just being equal human beings, knowing that we still have a very long way to go."

QUESTIONS

THERE ARE many questions still to be posed and answered about Nelson Mandela's extraordinary life. Future historians will reveal new documents and suggest different interpretations than the ones we have today. So-called "revisionists" will seek to debunk our current understandings as well, and some may be far less celebratory. For example, a new book "reveals" that Mandela was a secret member of the Communist Party, a claim his enemies have made over the years. He still denies it.

The Nelson Mandela Centre of Memory is besieged each month with thousands of emails and letters from all over the world. Curiously, the most frequently asked questions are most often the most basic ones about the long life he's led and the contribution he has made. Here are some of the Frequently Asked Questions and the Centre's responses. For more FAQs and responses, check out NelsonMandela.org.

Q: How can I contact Mr. Nelson Mandela?

A: Mr. Mandela retired from public life in 2004. You can, however, send him a message through the Nelson Mandela Centre of Memory at nmf@nelsonmandela.org.

Q: Who are Mr. Mandela's biological family?

A: Mr. Mandela has a big family. He had two daughters and two sons with his first wife, Evelyn Mase, and two daughters with his second wife, Winnie Madikizela. Only three of his children are still alive, daughters: Makaziwe, Zenani and Zindzi. He also has seventeen grandchildren and twelve surviving great-grandchildren. He has four step-children through his marriage to Graça Machel.

Q: Why does Mr. Mandela hold photo opportunities with certain people and not with others?"

A: All visitors are asked to sign a code of conduct agreeing that photographs taken with Mr. Mandela are for their private collections and should not be used for publication, fund-raising, or commercial purposes. From time to time Mr. Mandela chooses to be photographed by the press at such meetings.

Q: How many marriages has Mr. Nelson Mandela had and to whom?

A: Mr. Mandela has been married three times. He was first married to Evelyn Ntoko Mase in 1944. They separated in 1955 and divorced in 1958. She died in 2004. They had two daughters and two sons. Their baby daughter, Makaziwe, died at the age of nine months in 1947. Their eldest son, Madiba Thembekile (Thembi), was killed in a car accident in 1969 when Mr. Mandela was in prison. He was not allowed to attend the funeral. Their second son, Makgatho Lewanika, died of an AIDS-related illness in 2005. In 1958 Mr. Mandela married Winifred Nomzamo Zanyiwe Madikizela. They had two daughters, Zenani and Zindziswa. They divorced in 1996. On his birthday in 1998, Mr. Mandela married Graça Machel. Mrs. Machel brought two children and two step-children into the marriage.

Q: How old is Mr. Nelson Mandela?
A: Mr. Mandela turned 95 on July 18, 2013.

Q: Does Mr. Mandela, the Nelson Mandela Centre of Memory, or any of the sister charities accept fees when he meets people or appears in public?
A: No. Mr. Mandela meets who he chooses to meet, with absolutely no fees involved. There is no such thing as money for Mr. Mandela's time.

Q: What was Mr. Nelson Mandela's vision during the apartheid era?
A: Mr. Mandela's vision during the apartheid era was for the eradication of apartheid. He envisioned a South Africa in which all its citizens had equal rights and where every adult would have the right to vote for the government of his/her choice.

Q: What was apartheid?
A: Apartheid was the official policy of the National Party, which came to power in 1948 in South Africa. It was the practice of offi-

cial racial segregation. Under apartheid everyone in South Africa had to be classified according to a particular racial group. This determined where someone could be born, where they could live, where they could go to school, where they could work, where they could be treated if they were sick and where they could be buried when they died. Only white people could vote and they had the best opportunities and the most money spent on their facilities. Apartheid made others live in poverty. Black South Africans' lives were strictly controlled. Many thousands of people died in the struggle to end apartheid.

Q: What were Mr. Nelson Mandela's achievements in jail?

A: Mr. Mandela was held in Robben Island Maximum Security Prison until 1982, after which he was transferred to Pollsmoor Prison and then to Victor Verster Prison, from which he was released on February 11, 1990. He withstood extremely harsh conditions in prison with dignity and fortitude. Other prisoners remark on how he became a leader of all the other prisoners, fighting for their rights to get better treatment, improved food, and study privileges. He encouraged fellow prisoners never to give away their dignity. He also became a unifier between prisoners belonging to different political organizations. In the latter part of his imprisonment, Mr. Mandela initiated talks with the apartheid regime, which ultimately led to peaceful negotiations in South Africa.

Q: What were the names of Mr. Nelson Mandela's parents?

A: Mr. Mandela's father was Chief (Nkosi) Mphakanyiswa Gadla Mandela. His mother was Nosekeni Fanny Mandela.

Q: What beliefs and actions influenced Mr. Nelson Mandela as a leader?

A: Mr. Mandela's actions were driven by an unshakable belief in the equality of all people and his determination to overthrow the racist system of apartheid. Mr. Mandela helped to organize and to lead many peaceful protest campaigns, but after many violent disruptions by the state, it became clear to him and his colleagues that the regime would not allow peaceful change. In 1961 they formed Umkhonto we Sizwe (Spear of the Nation)—also known as MK—as an army for freedom fighters and launched the armed struggle.

Q: What were the dates of Mr. Nelson Mandela's prison time?

A: Mr. Mandela was arrested on several occasions and stood trial four times. On July 30, 1952, he and nineteen of his comrades were arrested for his role in the Defiance Campaign and stood trial in September 1952. He and the nineteen others were found guilty on December 2 for "statutory Communism"—which the apartheid regime used to define people who opposed its laws. Their sentence was nine months in jail with hard labor, suspended for five years. On December 5, 1956, Mr. Mandela and others were arrested on charges of High Treason. They were released on bail about two weeks later.

At the end of the four-and-a-half year trial, charges were withdrawn against all the accused. On March 29, 1961, Mr. Mandela and twenty-nine colleagues were found to be innocent of the charges laid against them. During the Treason Trial the African National Congress was outlawed and Mr. Mandela began operating secretly after the end of the trial. Later that year, Umkhonto we Sizwe, the armed wing of the ANC, was formed. Mr. Mandela left the country at the beginning of 1962 for military training and to gather support for the ANC. He was arrested in South Africa on August 5, 1962, and charged with inciting people to strike and for leaving the country without a passport. He was convicted and on November 7, 1962, he was sentenced to five years in jail. He was sent to Robben Island Maximum Security Prison in May 1963. But in July 1963 he was brought to Pretoria to stand trial for sabotage in what became known as the Rivonia Trial. Most of the accused in that trial had been arrested at Liliesleaf farm in a suburb of Johannesburg called Rivonia. That trial started in October 1963, and on June 11, 1964, eight of the nine accused were convicted of sabotage. The next day they were sentenced to life imprisonment.

Q: When was Mr. Nelson Mandela released from prison?

A: Sunday, February 11, 1990.

Q: What does the name 'Madiba' mean?

A: Madiba is the name of the Thembu clan to which Mr. Mandela belongs. It gets its name from a nineteenth-century Thembu chief. All the members of this clan can also be called Madiba. Mr. Mandela is called Madiba as a sign of both respect and affection.

Q: Did Mr. Nelson Mandela go to a multiracial school?

A: No. When Mr. Mandela went to school, there were no schools that children of different races could attend together. When he attended the University of the Witwatersrand, however, he was in a mixed-race law class.

Q: How do you pronounce Graça Machel?

A: Gra-ssa Ma-shell.

Q: How many brothers does Mr. Nelson Mandela have?

A: Mr. Mandela's father had four wives and a total of thirteen children. With Mr. Mandela's mother, Nosekeni, he had four children: Mr. Mandela and three daughters. So Mr. Mandela had three full sisters, three half-brothers, and six half-sisters.

Q: How many people did Mr. Nelson Mandela free?

A: The liberation movements freed all the people of South Africa, which had a population of approximately 40 million.

Q: Is the quote about "deepest fear" something that Mr. Mandela said?

A: No. This is a quote by an American author named Marianne Williamson and it has been incorrectly attributed to Mr. Mandela.

Q: How tall is Mr. Mandela?

A: 1.94-metres, or 6.3 feet.

Q: What books can I buy for my children to read about Mr. Mandela?

A: *Long Walk to Freedom: The Autobiography of Nelson Mandela*, *The Illustrated Long Walk to Freedom* (children's version) abridged by Chris van Wyk, *Nelson Mandela: The Authorized Comic Book*.

RECOGNITION

IN HIS Nobel Peace Prize acceptance speech, Mandela thanked "these countless human beings, both inside and outside our country [who] had the nobility of spirit to stand in the path of tyranny and injustice, without seeking selfish gain. They recognized that an injury to one is an injury to all and therefore acted together in defense of justice and a common human decency."

When he is honored, Mandela invariably says he believes that the honor is really intended for all who fought for and achieved freedom in South Africa. After a ticker-tape parade in New York, he told me all the adulation was really for the African National Congress. But if the ANC held a parade in Lower Manhattan without Mandela, would anyone come?

Mandela's is among the most recognized faces and names in the world. A nuclear particle has been named after him, as well as a plant. The number of awards he has won, and streets, schools, and even towns named after him are legion. And yet, as his lifelong friend and lawyer George Bizos has told me, Mandela doesn't want statutes erected in his memory, or streets named after him. The legacy he would like most of all is in the changed circumstances of people, in improved lives, in freedom and the ability of people everywhere to enjoy the freedom they have gained. Bizos added that if someone has money and wants to honor Madiba, he should build a school or a clinic, something that will directly improve people's lives.

IF I MUST choose one quality in Mandela that has outshone all the others, it is indeed his ability to recognize the moment in which he finds himself and then to outfit himself accordingly.

Speaking of the Defiance Campaign, biographer Anthony Sampson told an interviewer that Mandela "had quite a strong touch of the showman, of course, which made some people, including myself, a bit skeptical [at first] about what really lay behind the show. . . . He was always a master of imagery. He always looked right for the part. That's true of most great politicians, incidentally, but it was most striking in his case. I remember when he launched the Defiance Campaign. He was the volunteer in chief, and there he was in a long military overcoat, supervising, looking every inch the . . . paramilitary man. Very imposing. The fact that he always looked right and that his smile, which was almost too good to be true, that wide, wide, smile."

Richard Stengel spoke of Mandela's ability to recognize and put into perspective the larger meaning of a situation, with reference to Mandela's recognition of what it was going to take to make the most of the Robben Island prison experience. Speaking to an interviewer for American public television, Stengel said the following:

One side of [his] maturity, one thing that he learned in prison, was you set your sights in the far distance, and he did. I am not sure that he was conscious of it in the very beginning. But fairly soon he was, when he decided to learn Afrikaans, when he decided that he needed to have some kind of relationship with those guards. In a strange way, he realized, and it may be [that he did so] unconsciously that the relationship between him and his Afrikaans guards was a microcosm for the whole South African experience. . . .

What we've been talking about . . . [is] the kind of lover's quarrel that he had with the world. The genius, in a strange way, of Nelson Mandela, is that he was able to transfer the personal to the political. We ordinary folk might feel personally angry, aggrieved if somebody does something to us, don't think about it in a larger context. He managed to, at some point, think about it all in a larger context, not take it personally.

And so, in a way, his greatest challenges came after his release, when he was recognized the world over for his achievements, yet was also in some ways most alone, especially after the heartbreaking separation and divorce from Winnie. He faced a completely new set of circumstances.

Mandela's longtime comrade Mac Maharaj, who most recently was the person who released medical updates on Mandela's health to the press, remembers how at the time of Mandela's release from prison, it wasn't Mandela's release that came as a surprise—since it was by then already anticipated—but the unbanning of the various banned organizations.

"There was only one element of surprise," Maharaj said, "and that was how the unbanning extended even to the Communist Party and Umkhonto we Sizwe. Now, how the hell does a liberation army operate when it is unbanned, when until that very moment your task was to wage war?"

STALWART

DURING HIS June 1990 tour of the United States, Nelson Mandela flew to Miami to speak to a union convention. It was a tense moment because anti-Castro Cubans protested, denouncing him as a Communist and a terrorist. SWAT squads were out in force wearing body armor and displaying automatic weapons while a small plane circled overhead towing a sign denouncing the ANC.

When interviewed, Mandela said he thought it was totally unreasonable for critics to bash him for his friendship with Cuba. "Fidel Castro supported us while we couldn't even get close to the American government," he explained. "Why should we criticize Cuba?"

Inside the convention, I spoke to a few black female delegates who started jumping up and down when he entered the hall.

"We love him," they screamed. "He's a stand-up leader when so many of our leaders sell us out."

In South Africa, the term "stalwart" might be interchangeable with "stand-up." Both refer to the idea of consistent leadership that endures for years, earning respect and admiration.

On his ninety-fourth birthday on July 18, 2012, the National Education, Health and Allied Workers Union used the term to call on its members to support what Mandela stood for: "This stalwart of our liberation never betrayed the struggle for freedom and did not waver in the face of danger. He sacrificed his

life and livelihood in search of justice for the oppressed and vulnerable. . . . The challenge for our leaders is to ensure that they
learn from him and they prioritize service delivery above their
personal interests and those of their families. The fight against
corruption should be intensified in order to protect the legacy of
stalwarts like Mandela and others who gave their all on behalf of
the oppressed without expecting anything in return."

HE WON accolades like this because Mandela always called attention to his organization, not himself. As Parliament Speaker Max
Sisulu noted in a Nelson Mandela lecture he gave in India: "[He]
never sought to place himself above others. He is a product of
our organization, his views were honed within the organization
and the dreams and aspirations he articulated were those shared
with his comrades in arms: Walter Sisulu, Govan Mbeki, Ahmed
Kathrada, Yusuf Dadoo, and many others. When he spoke, he
spoke for them all."

SOME OF the best insights into Mandela's character have come
from people like Ahmed Kathrada, who worked alongside him in
the movement, then in prison.

Kathy told me, "I first met him in 1945 or '46. I would say
that prison brings out the best and the worst in people. It's a real
test. There are, what do you call it, things that happen in prison,
temptations in prison that one can take advantage of.

"First of all, when we came to prison, to Robben Island, he
said, 'Chaps, we are no longer leaders. We don't make policy, we
don't give instructions. Our leaders are outside the country.' In
the first years it was Chief Luthuli. After he died, it was Thabo

Mbeki and others. 'Those are our leaders,' he said. 'Here we are ordinary prisoners. No preferential treatment.' I mean, he didn't have to tell us but he did, and he practiced that in prison.

"There was also apartheid between Indians and coloreds on the one side and Africans on the other, and the most glaring example was that for ten years the Africans did not have bread. We had bread. I mean clothing, too. They were given short trousers; we were given long trousers. He was offered equal treatment with us. He refused.

"And when I talk about our leadership as a whole, we did pick and shovel work. It was very hard. We got used to it after a while. He was exempted. He refused such special treatment. In 1977, after being in prison for thirteen years, he was offered release, provided he would go to the Transkei. He refused. In 1985, all of us were offered release on certain conditions. Now by that time we were at Pollsmoor, five of us. It didn't take us any debate: we told Madiba to write a letter and tell them we are not accepting this release."

Kathy is impatient with the idea that anyone would ever suggest Mandela was anything other than a stand-up, stalwart leader. "They don't know. You see, unfortunately, there's an increase today, particularly among ignorant people, who think the revolution was just around the corner and everything was going to be all right without negotiations. What they forget is that the South African Army was the strongest in the whole of Africa. They could literally walk through Africa without resistance because the [liberated] African countries were few, so there was no army in Africa that was as strong as this one.

"Madiba's timing was just perfect, otherwise there would have been so much more bloodshed. But people don't know those things. People don't know what the White Right Wing—not the lunatic fringe like Terre'Blanche of the neo-Nazi AWB, but the generals leading the South African Army—what they were planning. Now they would never have defeated us. I mean, we were going to win. Everything was turning in our favor. The people in South Africa were becoming more and more politicized. The international community was isolating apartheid, so everything was in our favor, but always with the idea that we would force the enemy to the negotiating table. That was the ANC policy."

THE DEBATE over Mandela's effectiveness as a negotiator and president will continue. But his willingness to stand up courageously when he believes it is the right thing to do is undeniable. For example, it took great courage for him to personally embrace AIDS activism even when his successor and former deputy president Mbeki became a symbol for those who didn't believe fighting AIDS should be a priority, stressing instead "diseases of poverty." Mandela helped reintroduce AIDS as a major human rights issue at speeches in South Africa and at international conferences, saying, "The more we lack the courage and the will to act, the more we condemn to death our brothers and sisters, our children and our grandchildren. When the history of our times is written, will we be remembered as the generation that turned our backs in a moment of a global crisis, or will it be recorded that we did the right thing?"

Elaine McKay, HIV/AIDS program manager at the foundation, said Mandela was gutsy enough to say he had made a mistake on the issue earlier:

"Mr. Mandela is the first leader I know who, as former president, was quite happy to get up and say, 'I'm sorry.' He said after his presidential years that he was so concerned with nation-building that he didn't pay sufficient attention to HIV and AIDS. When the Nelson Mandela Foundation was then set up, he was clear that he wanted it to be a clear priority for the foundation to correct what he could have done during the presidential years. HIV was going to be one of his top priorities."

The foundation would soon be criticized for spending too much time on AIDS, for turning Mandela into an AIDS activist.

McKay explained: "It affected him personally. He lost a child. So for him it wasn't about politics. It was about doing the right thing. And that's what inspired me when I worked with Nelson Mandela. He came up and he said, 'My son died, and he died of AIDS.' He didn't hide it.

"He said, 'For all of you who think that this disease is a three-letter sickness, you've created terms that take away from the seriousness of the disease. I've lost a child. Don't allow the silence around the disease to kill our people.' He broke the silence. What better leader to be associated with: one that makes it personal and makes it real. That level of integrity is unprecedented today."

When AIDS activist Zackie Achmat of the Treatment Action Campaign in South Africa announced he would stop taking his medicine because they were unaffordable for poor South Africans, Mandela called and appealed to him to take his medicine. Achmat said no, but they later met and Mandela threw his considerable weight and visibility behind him and his campaign. The controversial activist and the respected leader became friends.

Mandela later called him a "national hero." On one occasion, when former president Thabo Mbeki refused to take Achmat's calls, Mandela broke all protocol and went personally to his home to try to persuade him on the issue.

Mandela later asked Bill Clinton to intervene with pharmaceutical companies, with the result that lower-cost AIDS drugs were made more widely available. Elaine MacKay admired Mandela's persistence on an issue he was not obligated to act on. "We were ridiculed [in some quarters]. Someone said to me, 'You took Mr. Mandela's number, prisoner number 46664, instead of prisoner to president, you made him prisoner to AIDS activist. We did get that criticism. But we had his mandate, and he was prepared to buffer the criticism that we encountered. So he honestly took a principled stand, and backed us up every step of the way, even when we were faced with political problems."

I asked Elaine to tell me what it was like for her to comfort Mandela when he was grieving privately for his dead child.

"I went to his home to sympathize with him, along with a colleague from the Mandela Foundation. We sat around his dining room table, and I couldn't find the words to say, 'I'm sorry,' you know? As parents we don't want to bury our children?

"He spoke of how he wasn't able to attend one of his kid's burials when he was imprisoned on Robben Island because they wouldn't give him a pass to leave. So it was in this context that he asked, 'Why didn't I know sooner? Is there something that I can do? Is there something our country can do better? What are all the other challenges other people are facing when you can't afford access to treatment?' For him, no one needed to die of AIDS. The fact that it was his son made it even more real for him.

It was so painful to watch, but all he wanted to know was, 'What are we going to do about it? How can we prevent this happening to somebody else?'

"It was so touching to watch. Because all you know is the Nelson Mandela that makes the hair on your arms stand up. The kind of man who can inspire fear by virtue of his size, and how he uses his voice. But he also has such a soft and gentle side that I've seen. That is also his legacy."

TERRORIST

What's the difference between a liberation movement and a band of terrorists? The simple answer . . . is point of view. Consider the African National Congress (ANC). During the long struggle against apartheid, what the Organisation of African Unity (OAU) saw as a liberation movement the racist minority government of South Africa labeled as terrorists. Ask one person in Washington and another in Riyadh today about Al Qaeda and you're bound to get the same diversity of opinion.

—SOUTH AFRICAN INSTITUTE OF INTERNATIONAL RELATIONS, 2004

NELSON MANDELA was not always loved; for years, many right-wingers and defenders of apartheid defamed and detested him as a terrorist, and several politicians went on record expressing such views:

"This hero worship is very much misplaced."—British Member of Parliament (MP) John Carlisle, on the BBC screening of the *Free Nelson Mandela* concert in 1990.

"The ANC is a typical terrorist organization. . . . Anyone who thinks it is going to run the government in South Africa is living in cloud-cuckoo land."—Former British Prime Minister Margaret Thatcher, 1987

"How much longer will the Prime Minister allow herself to

be kicked in the face by this black terrorist?"—British MP Terry
Dicks, mid-1980s
    "Nelson Mandela should be shot."—British MP Teddy Taylor,
mid-1980s

UNDER THE terms of South Africa's Suppression of Communism
Act, and as a result of the conviction at the Rivonia Trial, Mandela was found guilty of sabotage, and the ANC was branded a
terrorist organization.
    Here are the charges Mandela faced:

- One count under the South African Suppression of Communism Act No. 44 (1950), charging that the accused
  committed acts calculated to further the achievement of
  the objective of Communism;
- One count of contravening the South African Criminal Law
  Act (1953), which prohibits any person from soliciting or
  receiving any money or articles for the purpose of achieving
  organized defiance of laws and country; and
- Two counts of sabotage, committing or aiding or procuring
  the commission of the following acts:

  1. The further recruitment of persons for instruction and
     training, both within and outside the Republic of South
     Africa, in:
     a) the preparation, manufacture and use of explosives—
        for the purpose of committing acts of violence and
        destruction in the aforesaid Republic, (the prepa-
        ration and manufacture of explosives, according to
        evidence submitted, included 210,000 hand grenades,

48,000 anti-personnel mines, 1,500 time devices, 144 tons of ammonium nitrate, 21.6 tons of aluminum powder and a ton of black powder);

b) the art of warfare, including guerrilla warfare, and military training generally for the purpose in the aforesaid Republic;

2. Further acts of violence and destruction (these include 193 counts of terrorism committed between 1961 and 1963);

3. Acts of guerrilla warfare in the aforesaid Republic;

4. Acts of assistance to military units of foreign countries when involving the aforesaid Republic;

5. Acts of participation in a violent revolution in the aforesaid Republic, whereby the accused, injured, damaged, destroyed, rendered useless or unserviceable, put out of action, obstructed with or endangered:

a) the health or safety of the public;

b) the maintenance of law and order;

c) the supply and distribution of light, power or fuel;

d) postal, telephone or telegraph installations;

e) the free movement of traffic on land; and

f) the property, movable or immovable, of other persons or of the state.*

Significantly, the people who worked with him then didn't see themselves as terrorists, but as part of a liberation struggle.

---

* Source: *The State v. Nelson Mandela et al.*, Supreme Court of South Africa, Transvaal Provincial Division, 1963–1964, Indictment.

ONCE THE ANC was banned, there were internal struggles as the activists reimagined themselves as an underground organization. Nelson Mandela called for a new underground structure in what was known as the "M Plan." In a 1986 book called *Apartheid's Rebels*, Stephen M. Davis, who had been with the US State Department explained: "The M Plan's intention was to wean the ANC away from dependence on characteristics of organization most vulnerable to governmental pressure. Mandela envisioned the construction of a discreet but firm cellular network at the grass roots level."

"It wasn't easy, and it wasn't always successful," recalled ANC veteran Mac Maharaj, the former Robben Island prisoner turned government minister and spokesperson. "We were all amateurs. We were learning as infants do how to live as outlaws, and so we made a lot of mistakes. We were terribly trusting with our own colleagues. We assumed that if you were arrested and you were interrogated and you were tortured, you could withstand it. Kathy is perhaps one of those who helped to write the rules in the Communist Party that if you were an arrested comrade and a tortured comrade, don't talk. This is not a sustainable thing under modern forms of torture. But when it comes to strategy, I think there is a lot of room, and I have not known a single struggle that has started off with a readymade strategy that went through [to the end]. Strategy has to change all the time. . . .

"We must not run ourselves down with criticisms of ourselves that we threw out the baby with the bathwater. All revolutions have this. Fidel Castro was asked whether if he was to live his life again, would he have carried the raid on the Moncada Barracks and he said, 'No.' But he also said, 'At that time it was the right thing to do.'"

IN SOUTH AFRICA, the armed struggle was undermined by naïveté and a lack of security. The "high command" met at farm called Liliesleaf, now a tourist museum, but then operated by the Communist Party in the leafy suburb of Johannesburg called Rivonia. It was there that the plans were being made and even weapons assembled for a sabotage campaign. It was also there that the police raided on July 11, 1963, sweeping up top leaders who were prosecuted in what became known as the Rivonia Trial. Nelson Mandela was not arrested with the others but he had been there and later joined the defendants.

In his book, *The Mission*, one of the men convicted of sabotage in the Rivonia Trial, Denis Goldberg, reveals that even the intelligence wing of the ANC government that has access to old files doesn't know or won't say where the leak was. "To this day, we are not sure how the police found us," he wrote. "We know that foreign agents were active because it is known that Nelson Mandela was betrayed by the American CIA in exchange for one of their South African operatives who had been arrested."

Overseas, Mandela's supporters rejected the terrorist designation, but not so his detractors. London's *Independent* reported, "In his autobiography, *Conflict of Loyalty*, former foreign secretary Sir Geoffrey Howe says that even as late as October 1987, at a press conference following the Commonwealth Heads of Government Conference in Vancouver, Mrs. Thatcher was quick to dismiss the African National Congress as "a typical terrorist organization." Sir Geoffrey added sadly: "Absolutism still held sway."

Years later, however, the BBC reported that when Ahmed Kathrada took Thatcher on a tour of Robben Island, he was surprised to hear her say that she believed her intervention had helped save his comrades' lives. Kathy said: "She assured me that she had played a positive role during our trial. We were expecting a death sentence. We were well aware that there was all sorts of pressure both from within South Africa and from abroad—pressure from people not necessarily agreeing with the ANC's policies, he said, but who didn't want the defendants to be turned into martyrs of the revolution. At the time, Mrs. Thatcher was a frontbench MP in Harold Macmillan's government. I'm not interested in whether she was prime minister or whatever. I have no reason to doubt what she was saying and it was good to hear she played a role."

South African writer Alan Paton testified in court that if the defendants were executed then the South African government would have no one to negotiate with. On the night before the judge's verdict, George Bizos was with Paton, who was staying at the home of British Consul General Leslie Minford, who had also been in British intelligence. Minford told them, after a night of hard drinking, that there would be no death sentence, according to the judge. Later, according to former Afrikaner government economist Sampie Terreblanche, British Ambassador Robin Renwick secretly pressed the government to release Mandela and his fellow ANC prisoners.

Nevertheless, Mandela's name remained on the US terrorism list for years, until nearly at the end of his presidential term and eighteen years after his release from prison. On July 1, 2008, NBC reported:

> This morning, President Bush signed into law a bill granting Secretary Rice the authority to waive travel restrictions on President Mandela and other members

of the African National Congress (ANC). The bill was sponsored by Democratic Sens. John Kerry and Sheldon Whitehouse, along with Republican Sen. Bob Corker.

The senators say Mandela and ANC members remained on the list "for activities they conducted against South Africa's apartheid regime decades ago." They also said in their written statement that the removal "end[s] an embarrassing impediment to improving US–South Africa relations."

On the occasion of the ANC's removal from the watch list rolls, *New York Times* columnist Nicholas Kristof commented:

Sometimes government officials become intoxicated by the counter-terrorism portfolio. Indeed, totally inebriated. To put it simply, they go nuts.

That's one explanation for Guantánamo, for torture memos, for the Iraq invasion. But of all the ridiculous things we did in the name of protecting American security, putting Nelson Mandela on a terrorism watch list may be the most absurd. Mandela, the symbol of peaceful conciliation, the former president of South Africa, the 90-year-old hero—what did we think he would do, strap on a suicide vest?

Even still, the question comes up, such as at the 2012 Conservative Political Action Conference. *Mother Jones* magazine reported on one of the conference sponsors:

As Right Wing Watch notes, one of the sponsors at February's conference [was] Youth For Western Civilization, a group dedicated to, as the name suggests, preventing the "extinction" of Western Civilization at the hands of multiculturalism. . . .

Among other things, the group is a passionate defender of South Africa's white heritage. A recent blog post featured at the site accuses the African National Congress, the nation's ruling party, of waging a "genocide" against Afrikaners, and pins much of the blame on revered former president Nelson Mandela.

So the issue of who and what is a terrorist remains a hotly contested and inflammatory one in the era of the war on terror. It does not belong to the past, but is still being debated today. Nelson Mandela's success and emergence as a global icon has not changed that.

UNKNOWN

THE MORE that is known about Nelson Mandela, the harder it is to identify the real person behind the different roles and personas.

Here is Madiba speaking of his first encounters with Joe Slovo and Ruth First, in a flat leased by Ismail Meer, said to be one of Ruth's lovers before she married Joe. Mandela wrote, "There we studied and even danced until the early hours of the morning, and it became a kind of headquarters for young freedom fighters."

I like this description of Nelson Mandela, so alive in his words, someone in love with life and the struggle for freedom, who saw that the two things, pleasure and struggle, went well together, studying and dancing until all hours with fellow freedom fighters.

Ruth's initial memory of Nelson as he was back then: "Good looking, very proud, very dignified, very prickly, rather sensitive, perhaps even arrogant. But, of course, he was exposed to all the humiliations."

Of his first encounters with Mandela, Joe Slovo, who would later become one of his closest friends and confidants, remembered that Mandela was very conscious "of his blackness."

WHAT ABOUT his enemies at the time? How did *they* see Nelson Mandela? Here is Niël Barnard, one of South Africa's intelligence chiefs, speaking on PBS's *Frontline* program:

We more and more came to the conclusion that the only answer would be to talk to the real leaders of this country. . . . From an intelligence perspective looking at the history, looking at the whole development of Mr. Mandela . . . it was quite clear that he had to play a pivotal role. . . . I would say as early as 1982–1983. . . . I started discussions with President Botha, the prime minister at the time, [insisting] that we have to find a negotiated settlement. We have to find a way out of increasing civil conflict. . . .

I must put it very bluntly that we . . . had one of the best intelligence evaluation capacities on the globe. Make no mistake, whatever the old man [meaning Mandela] might write in his book about our knowledge [of the inner workings of] the ANC, we were absolutely well informed about what was going on within the ANC, what leadership was all about, what the personalities were all about, what the real power base within the inner corridors of power were. . . .

According to our assessment, there was just no question whatsoever that the towering . . . personality at the time [was Mandela]. . . . He was the symbol of keeping on with this whole process, of not giving up, of being a leader on the island, and taking the process forward. People released from the island like Mac Maharaj and others . . . the way in which they viewed the leadership of Mr. Mandela was quite clear from a real intelligence perspective. . . . Mr. Mandela was, by any real evaluation of the facts, by far the most important leader.

And yet, Barnard and his team were puzzled by Mandela, by the contradictions of his personality: "Mr. Mandela is one of those strange individuals. . . . He certainly is not the most charismatic public speaker that anybody has ever seen. He can be quite dreary, I would even say. But still, he has this strange charisma. [He is] a man people want to listen to. . . . So there was, in our minds, looking from an intelligence perspective, never the slightest doubt. This [was] the man—if you cannot find settlement with him, any settlement will be out."

SO WE are still, all of us, searching for Nelson Mandela. There is still much about him that is not widely known, or if known, not well understood. His birth name, Rolihlahla, means "troublemaker."

The name he was given by a schoolteacher—a common practice for Africans attending English schools, was Nelson, after Lord Nelson, a British colonial hero. His friends then shortened it to "Nel" or "Nelly."

"Tata" is the isiXhosa name for "father" and is a term of endearment that many South Africans use for Mr. Mandela. Since he is a father figure to many, they call him Tata regardless of their own age.

He is often called "Khulu," which means great, paramount, grand. Addressing Mandela this way is like calling him, "Great One." It is also a shortened form of the isiXhosa word "ubawomkhulu" for "grandfather."

"Dalibhunga" is the name Mandela was given at age sixteen, once he had undergone initiation, the traditional Xhosa rite of passage into manhood. It means "creator or founder of the council" or "convenor of the dialogue." The correct use of this name when greeting Mr. Mandela is "Aaah! Dalibhunga."

Of course, members of Mandela's family use many terms of endearment for him. His grandchildren use variants of "Grandfather," like "Granddad" for instance. His wife, Graça Machel, frequently calls him "Papa." Movement activists often refer to him as "the old man."

MANDELA MOVES with equal serenity in the worlds of the suites and the streets. He became the secretary of the International Club in Johannesburg and hosted multicultural evenings there. He is also, according to Cambridge University's Elleke Boehmer, on first-name terms with a number of Johannesburg gang leaders: to them, he speaks a local patois, "a broken mix of Afrikaans, Zulu, and Chicago-ese called *tsotsitaal.*"

NELSON MANDELA was emphatically an actor in real life, more than he was an actor of the stage, although he performed as Abraham Lincoln in one play and portrayed Creon in Sophocles' *Antigone* in a prison production.

One of the books he turned to in prison was *The Complete Works of William Shakespeare.* And on December 16, 1977, Mandela underlined a passage in *Julius Caesar* that reads: "Cowards die many times before their deaths. / The valiant never taste of death but once. / Of all the wonders that I yet have heard, / It seems to me most strange that men should fear, / seeing death, a necessary end will come when it will come."

Perhaps Elleke Boehmer put it best when she wrote in her book on Mandela that he was a stage actor, but one whose best performance was in real life where "as a performer and manipulator of images," he invented his own character.

"His performances were composed with a remarkable degree of self-knowledge," she wrote. "He was never unaware of the power of making a physical statement of the efficacy, whether in public or private, of masks; of how his life might be read as a model for African upward mobility and political success." She argued he had a "shrewd ability to manipulate his own myth."

IN HER BOOK, *Higher Than Hope*, Fatima Meer has quoted Mandela about what she calls his "dandy days," when he joined an "upper crust of African society who went ballroom dancing in black suit and tie."

"We spent hours practicing fox trots and waltzes, each of us taking turns leading and following," Mandela recalled.

But most of the places where he could show off his talents were out of bounds. The Mandela who had to submit to such indignities is the one we know least well, so complete has been his triumph over them.

VOICES RAISED UP IN SONG

MANDELA'S taste in music is eclectic, with a soft spot for the traditional sounds of his childhood and of his manhood before prison. His dancing onstage in later years has touched millions and seems to connect to the deep joy he feels because of the freedom struggle to which he has devoted, some would say sacrificed, his life—his celebration of how far the struggle for freedom has come under his guidance.

VUSI MAHLASELA still lives in the township of Mamelodi, outside Pretoria. He wrote a poem at age eleven that was later made into a hit song. He is widely celebrated as a folksinger, world troubadour, poet, and activist. The title track from Mahlasela's first album, "When You Come Back," released in 1992, instantly became an antiapartheid anthem, and Vusi soon became known as "The Voice."

> *This is the unknown grave*
> *The one who died maintaining his might*
> *His will being so strong and musically inclined*
> *His sad melodies coming out like smoke from the wood fire*
> *And he sang*
> *Mayibuye iAfrica, Sing now Africa*
> *Sing loud, sing to the people*

Vusi explained, "It all started around 1976. 'When You Come Back' was the poem I wrote, dedicating it to the people who left the country to enlist in the fight against the evil monster of apartheid. But it was a celebration of life as well, expressing the fears of those who left the country and then maybe yearned to come back home. When they come back home, will they still find their families, what will the country be like, will there be jobs and so on?"

> *This is the unknown grave*
> *The one who died maintaining his mind*
> *His will had been so strong and musically inclined*
> *His sad melody is coming out like smoke from the wood fire.*

Vusi's song excited audiences at the World Cup in South Africa and worldwide on TV:

> *Sing loud, sing to the people*
> *Let them give something to the world and not just take*
>   *from it*
> *Africa sing*

Vusi told me about the ideas behind the poem he wrote that became the hit song, saying, "You know, it does not take, doesn't only take from the world, but also gives something. There's more about emphasizing that gift of humanity as well that we have learned from our grandfathers, and a few like Nelson Mandela, Bishop Tutu, and the likes of Gandhi as well, who taught us that there is wisdom in forgiveness, and so on. But one thing which is more to my liking about these leaders, as well, is that they show the power, how when our leaders have the power, they can use it in a more positive way."

ZOLANI MKIVA is a royal poet, traditional artist, and praise singer who also recited for and alongside Mandela. Ukubonga (praise singing) is an art form revered in the Xhosa culture. He is also an actor in *Mandela: Long Walk to Freedom.*

Zolani told me about what Mandela means to him. "When even his face was not allowed to be published or to be seen, I had a picture in my mind of Madiba, and it's a great picture. You know the picture that you imagine is the greatest portrait that you can have, and it gives you the power to unleash the most powerful words describing something that you only see in your imagination. So it's the power of the imagination. But when you imagine something about a man who has sacrificed so much for his people that he was even prepared to lay his life down if need be, you know, we grew up with that kind of an atmosphere about him. So the praises I sang about Nelson Mandela at the time when I was at high school, when they were describing, defining, telling us about . . . For me, the coming back of the Messiah meant the release of Nelson Mandela, and him coming back to lead us."

Mandela met Zolani and asked him to accompany him on a speaking tour. Zolani became his opening act. Madiba was so impressed with him that he also invited him to perform at his inauguration on May 10, 1994.

"To be at the center of the inauguration on the tenth of May, 1994, was the most intimidating event for me that I've ever imagined. On the ninth, the night before, I couldn't sleep. All the time I had been reciting and rendering items at rallies and so on, so I didn't have a problem. I never scratched my head. I never broke my jaws. You give me a microphone and I go to town. But I was intimidated so much that night that I couldn't go to sleep because I was thinking, 'What do I say? How is it going to look? It's the first of its kind and it's the time and the moment when we are going to feel, touch, see freedom and Nelson Mandela taking over the reigns. What do I say? What do I do? How do I do it?

"I told myself that I'm going to take it to the basics and tell the world who Nelson Mandela is and it was as simple as saying: Nguye lo ke uMandela. Thwele leziswe zaseAfrica. besiwajongile. Yiyo le inkonyane eyohlanga. Zahlokoma iziswe zonke zehlabathi zimkhahlele uMandela. Zisithi halala Mandela halala.

"Basically, I was saying: There, Mandela. There is Mandela. There is the son of the soil. He has no perfumed lips. He speaks the truth. He has no cat eyes but he can see the true colors of the universe. He has no dog nose but he can smell and distinguish between carbon monoxide and oxygen. He has no donkey ears but he can hear what makes sense and what is a nuisance. He is the son of the soil, a brother to the daughters of the land.

"Halala Mandela halala."

I said: "I was in the crowd and saw Africans cry when they heard you recite, even as Mandela and Thabo Mbeki smiled. It was a demonstration of the power of art, the power of poetry, and the power that you unleashed, to use one of your favorite words."

Zolani expects the movie of *Long Walk to Freedom* to have the same effect:

"This film will play a role that has been lacking all this time. There is a great gap because we always import—even that which goes through our own national television for transmission to our own population. This movie gives us an opportunity to ensure that we engender a particular perspective, educate our youth through cinema, carrying content that flows from our own history. The movie is an opportunity for us to do that.

"We can no longer afford a situation where our youth are totally unaware and ignorant of their own history. We run a risk of going back to some of the things that happened if we don't ensure that our history is in the hearts and minds of our youth."

WAITING

FOR SOME it seemed shorter than the twenty-seven-and-a-half years he actually spent in prison, but for others it seemed to go on forever.

When he and his comrades first arrived on "The Island," as the Robben Island Maximum Prison was called, they were told they would only leave in a box. Visits were rare and highly supervised and controlled, as Winnie Mandela soon discovered.

The word "harsh" understates the reality. Consider going ten years without hot water, and you get the idea. Even as Mandela worked to build bridges to his warders, the power equation was simple. They had it, and the prisoners, with some exceptions in times of protest, didn't. The prisoners themselves settled in for the long wait.

It was only after Mandela left Robben Island for Pollsmoor Prison in 1982 that he was able to talk to the government, though, at first, secretly. He wasn't really negotiating. The two sides were feeling each other out.

But then as South Africa's economy took a dive, as the insurrection in the townships continued, and as overseas pressure built, the leadership in the South African government realized that they had to make changes. Under pressure from conservatives like Ronald Reagan and Margaret Thatcher—even as they branded the ANC a terrorist organization—the ice started to melt.

F. W. de Klerk has said that he had been initially unaware of the secret talks but that soon changed: "I was not aware of what was happening behind the scenes until I became the leader of my party exactly one year before I made the speech of the second of February, 1990. On the second of February, '89, I was elected leader, when P. W. Botha resigned not as president, but as leader of the National Party.

"From that moment onwards I was briefed, because having been elected leader of the governing party made me sort of president-elect. It was a great advantage not to be president but to have time to prepare oneself for when you become president. Already, before I became president, I've come to the conclusion that the tentative negotiations which took place behind the scenes were worthwhile. That a negotiated solution was what South Africa needed, and that that could not take place without the release of Nelson Mandela and all other political prisoners."

From time to time, reports of something about to happen leaked out, leading to a flurry of rumors, headlines, and anticipation. By the late '80s, it felt as if the wait was ending but, like his predecessors, de Klerk worried about what he told me was a "real threat from Communists." But then, glasnost broke out in the Soviet Union.

"Fundamental changes were taking place and being planned. In the end, I could not have put together the package which I announced on the second of February, 1990, if the Berlin Wall did not come down. That created for us a window of opportunity. Suddenly the threat of Communist expansionism in South Africa lost the sting in its tail. Suddenly it was no longer credible. And that helped me greatly to take the initiatives that I took."

When I told South African businessman and former union leader Cyril Ramaphosa that de Klerk said his party could have "held on for another ten or fifteen years," Ramaphosa shook his head with a look on his face that said de Klerk was crazy if he really thought so.

Critics of de Klerk say that even as he credits himself and his colleagues for releasing Mandela, they were under pressure from overseas by threats of escalating bank withdrawals and sanctions. Former banker and activist Terry Crawford-Browne, who worked with Archbishop Tutu, explained to me that de Klerk and company were being squeezed: "That pushed him into a corner. He was trying to distance himself from P. W. Botha, but the first couple of weeks after he came to office were amongst the bloodiest we faced in 1989, which is what led to the March for Peace, led by the archbishop. I think that de Klerk thought that Nelson Mandela would be a six-month wonder. He would then remove the most offensive aspects of apartheid, install a puppet, but then resurrect the essentials of apartheid."

De Klerk acted when Parliament opened on February 2. He announced that the ANC and other banned groups and parties would be unbanned, and that Mandela and other political leaders would be freed—but he didn't at first announce the date.

The waiting continued.

Mail & Guardian journalist Pippa Green reported what happened next when activists who had formed a Mandela Release Committee, and who were planning his welcome, were invited to a private meeting.

"Trevor Manuel got a message from the office of General Johan Willemse, the commissioner of prisons. So did Dullah Omar. So did Bulelani Ngcuka. They passed it on to Saki Macozoma, a young South African Council of Churches activist who was visiting the Western Cape. Could they be at the HF Verwoerd Building in the parliament complex—the Cape Town offices of the Cabinet—at 2:30 PM?"

Trevor Manual's wait was almost over. He told me:

"I was part of the UDF [United Democratic Front] delegation that saw Madiba on the Friday, the ninth. I got a call early on the Saturday morning from de Klerk's office asking me to be there. And there were four of us there, and we were told that Madiba was going to be released on the Sunday, the eleventh. Then, we went to see him on the Saturday evening, the day before his release. He was cool, completely cool. Fully in control."

In *Long Walk to Freedom*, Mandela wrote about the big day this way: "The momentousness of an occasion is lost in the welter of a thousand details."

He recalled, "I awoke on the day of my release after only a few hours' sleep. . . . I did a shortened version of my usual exercise regimen, washed, and ate breakfast. I then telephoned a number of people from the ANC and the UDF in Cape Town to come to the cottage to prepare for my release and work on my speech."

He also prepared to receive a flood of visitors and his wife Winnie, who was flying down from Johannesburg. His "check-out" time was 3:00 PM.

Madiba's days of waiting were drawing rapidly to a close.

Rob Nixon writes that, "During the countdown to February 11, 'Waiting for Mandela' became a routine deadline, reinforcing a very South African preoccupation with imminent time. In their distinctive ways, the nation's black and white cultures seek obsessively through metaphors of dawn, birth, revolutionary redemption with apocalyptic and historical culture."

Where were the top officials of the ANC while their leader was readying himself for the biggest news event of his life? Thabo Mbeki sheepishly recounted a screw-up that kept him away in this surprising exchange:

"We knew that he was going to be released because we had been involved in the negotiations with the representatives of the government. It was planned. We knew it and arranged with the people, our interlocutors in the South African government, that they would telephone me in Lusaka to indicate the exact date of the release. And we had agreed on a code.

"But then I had to go to England. So I spoke to my wife and I said look, somebody might phone and say the following. . . . Told her what the code was without explaining what it meant. If you get such a message, please convey it immediately to me in London.

"The message came to her, in Lusaka. She passed it onto a friend of mine in England who didn't understand it. 'It's going to rain tomorrow.'

"It [didn't sound] particularly urgent. So she held onto it for three or four days, and in the end, she passed it on. Which was really basically a few hours before Madiba was to be released. . . . So, we would have had a number of days of forewarning about this, except that we had this breakdown in communication. The representatives of the government kept their promise—that as soon as the date was known they would convey it to us. But then on our side, we hadn't prepared."

FORMER LABOR leader Jay Naidoo was among the first to arrive at the house where Mandela was staying on the grounds of Victor Verster Prison, very early in the morning.

"They took us there, and I remember arriving at the door, and we walk in, and there's Mandela," he recalls with enthusiasm.

"Oh, comrades, how are you doing? Come in, come in."

"You know, he's welcoming us and there are my expectations, well I don't know what I was expecting actually. Because the last photograph we had seen of him was as a boxer, a pretty sturdy boxer. And here's this elegant, regal, towering man walking out with his hand outstretched to shake our hands, saying, 'Welcome.' And, you know, so yes, we were floored by it. He went out of his way to make us feel at home."

"Do you care to have some coffee or some tea? Come and sit down."

"And then he said, 'No, before you sit, let me take you around my house.' So he took us from room to room to show us the space. He showed us where the microphones were, and where he ate, and where he ate breakfast. It was the most wonderful meeting—like, I never met my grandfathers but I always expected that if I did, that would be like the morning I would have. Having tea and talking about things.

"And we didn't talk about the release or anything. For the first hour we just chatted about life. So that was my first experience of him."

While the world was waiting for Mandela, Mandela was waiting for his wife who was running late. Naidoo was sent to the airport to get her. He recalled that she would soon throw a verbal hand grenade into the gathering.

"An intense debate broke out about where should Mandela speak first. And this debate just went on for hours. Winnie was saying he should first speak in Jo'burg. Jo'burg was the political epicenter of the political struggle. You cannot speak in Cape Town first.

"And he's going around, making sure people have a biscuit,

they have some tea, cups are full. Doesn't say anything, you know? It's getting past the time that we've announced to the world that he's coming out and the world is waiting for him to come out. And here we are having tea and biscuits. So it was a most amazing thing."

Archbishop Tutu got wind of the debate and panicked. He feared that Cape Town would be destroyed if Mandela did not show up at the parade downtown, where tens of thousands had already been waiting for hours. He phoned one of Mandela's lawyers, Dullah Omar, to press him to stay on schedule.

Mandela then resolved the issue, saying, "Okay. I've heard all sides now. Let me say what I think. I've been here in Cape Town for twenty-seven years. My view is that this is the first place I should make my speech, because this has been my home for so long."

That ended the debate.

Winnie and Nelson, hand in hand, waited no longer.

PIPPA GREEN reported in the *Mail & Guardian* on what else was going on behind the scenes that explained why Mandela was so late in getting to Cape Town, where his enthusiastic supporters were waiting in the hot sun.

> Winnie . . . refused to get on the same plane as Murphy Morobe [of the United Democratic Front] (UDF) because he had distanced the movement from her. . . .
>
> So they chartered two planes instead of one. But they were propeller planes, not jets. . . . So the Johannesburg contingent boarded the "slowest plane in the world" that took four, not two, hours to reach Cape Town.

By then, the crowd in Cape Town had been waiting for hours. Restless young people already challenging the police and looting. Reported Green:

> It was now well past 3pm. Still Mandela didn't arrive. An angry murmur went through the swelling crowd that this was all a trick by de Klerk to confuse the oppressed masses.
>
> At 4.15pm Nelson Mandela finally walked out of Victor Verster Prison, an hour-and-a-quarter behind schedule, 27 years after he was first arrested at a road-block outside Pietermaritzburg.
>
> . . . A newspaper reported afterwards that Mandela's cavalcade had "roared" into the city just after 5.20pm. A huge crowd ran wildly alongside his car as it wound through the city, beating on the windows and chanting. A group of women jostled and pushed, desperate to see their leader.
>
> They wept and laughed simultaneously. The press of the crowd slowed the motorcade to jogging pace and Mandela, in the back seat with his wife Winnie, looked out at the mad crush of faces. He was impassive, with his fist raised stiffly in salute.

Though Mandela seemed impassive, his driver panicked when surrounded by a crowd. He was told by police to get out of the area and ended up in Rondebosch West, a suburb near the University of Cape Town. They pulled up outside a house to wait some more until they reconnected with their leadership—Trevor Manuel, Cyril Ramaphosa, Valli Moosa, and Jay Naidoo—who were in a panic because they had "lost" Mandela.

Green continued:

> A woman who had been watching the release on TV
> looked out in astonishment. The man she had just seen
> walking out of jail was now here outside her house. . . .
>
> About 6pm a traffic cop near the City Hall beckoned
> Manuel and said there was "someone who wanted to talk to
> him" on his two-way radio. It was a colonel in the security
> police whom Manuel knew from his frequent detentions.
>
> He said: "Trevor, you must go fetch Mandela. If you
> don't bring him here the city will burn down and hun-
> dreds of people are going to be killed. Go fetch him!"

When their party finally retrieved "their charge," he was
having tea with his shoes off with a local activist, this time in
Rondebosch East.

Trevor Manuel told me that Mandela looked up when the relieved
retinue rushed into the house. He asked, "Where were you chaps?
Lets do this thing, referring to the speech the world was waiting for."

Green concluded, "This time they got him into the City Hall
through its back entrance. US civil rights leader Jesse Jackson
was also there waiting. He had parked his car in front of the
building but it had been crushed by the crowd that climbed on
top of it to get a better view. He said at the time, "Mandela is still
not free because he still can't vote."

At dusk, Mandela got ready to address the restless crowd when
one more wrinkle surfaced. He suddenly realized he had left his
glasses in prison. Fortunately, Winnie had some spectacles and
he tried them on. They worked, and then he read his collectively

written speech, punctuated by freedom movement phrases like "Amandla!" (Power!) and "Mayibuye i Africa" (Come back Africa!) all of which electrified the crowd before him, as well as millions more around the world.

"I stand here before you today not as a prophet but as a humble servant of the people," he said in part. "Your tireless and heroic sacrifices have made it possible for me to be here today. I therefore place the remaining years of my life in your hands."

Some of his supporters would later criticize his speech for being too populist and not laying out a program. According to Anthony Sampson, Margaret Thatcher, de Klerk, and the then government were "disappointed" because he didn't distance himself from the ANC and the armed struggle.

It was a miracle that more people were not hurt in the crush and chaos of the events. Mandela gave his speech from a tiny platform hanging off the City Hall building. He shouted into the microphone, indicating that he had no idea how sound could now be amplified, a technology that had evolved since he had been imprisoned.

"He was shouting into the mic," Ramaphosa told me with a smile. "I kept having to move it away from his mouth."

Pippa Green then had an even better capper: "The following day, after nearly 48 hours without sleep, Manuel collapsed into bed at around midnight after the rally only to be awoken at 4am by a phone call from Mandela. 'Trevor, where are my weights?' asked the old man."

What a story! It can truly be seen as vindication of the aphorism, "All things come to those who wait."

X FACTOR

THROUGHOUT his biography of Mandela, Anthony Sampson makes the point again and again, citing events and interventions, that global pressure was the X factor, the secret sauce, in bringing down apartheid and supporting the domestic struggles of South Africans.

There's a parochialism in South Africa, born of its geography on the southern tip of the continent, and perhaps thanks to the years of isolation and sanctions that made many of the white people who lived there feel like a people apart. White Africans were given to the same tribal parochialism of any others, shaped by their culture and the dictates of their language. Afrikaans speakers lived in their own bubble influenced by their history, the Dutch Reformed Church, and racial codes. Like many distinct cultures, individuals often had limited contacts with others.

Even as many South Africans think of their history as all their own doing—warts, wars triumphs and all—their country was never, to quote the Scottish poet John Donne, "an island unto itself." Decisions made elsewhere have always shaped its dynamic history.

There was colonialism. There was imperialism. There were the Dutch, the British, the Anglo-Boer War, the mining companies and a blood fest from day one over who would rule the land and who would serve those who ruled. You can say that this isn't the time for us to revisit all the pain from the old days, except that the pain of the old hasn't yet gone away in the new.

When the ANC mounted its armed struggle and some of its leaders fled the country, they opened up what they called an "external mission."

At first it was based in London and then in Dar Es Salaam, Tanzania, on a street named for sub-Saharan Africa's first independent president, Kwame Nkrumah. Nelson Mandela's law partner Oliver Tambo was in charge, and he worked from morning until night directing the movement and producing propaganda.

Mosie Moola, one of his South African comrades who joined him there, told me that on the days that Tambo published a report on developments in South Africa, he would stay up all night to get it out, often sleeping on the floor.

Sue Rabkin, an English radical, would later work in Zambia and Mozambique in the ANC's underground war. She said, "We set up propaganda units. The first and most important thing was to erect some kind of a basic structure. It had to be a secret structure, so everybody couldn't know what the next person was doing, which made life very difficult. We had to make sure everyone had heard of the ANC, that they knew what the ANC stood for, so we produced cassettes, which were produced by our informational public city department, which we then smuggled into the country. We gave them to taxi drivers etc. So people traveling on a combi would hear, 'This is the voice of the ANC,' and then they'd hear these sort of gunshots. And we had to say what we stood for, so there was that whole aspect of keeping the movement alive. Part of which was enhanced by our military operations. Everybody had code names. My children used to call them cold names. . . . But I didn't have one. There weren't that many whites so it, you know, there wasn't much point."

The external mission was there to serve the internal movement whose leaders were jailed or banned. In those days, the ANC would send its recruits mostly to "Socialist" countries— that's what they called themselves—seeking money, military training, and support.

Not surprisingly, the American Central Intelligence Agency was also monitoring the support given to the ANC by the Eastern bloc, as well as spying on the ANC. In June 1963, the *New York Times* reported, "CIA Tie Reported in Mandela Arrest." It quoted an unnamed CIA official as boasting, "We have turned Mandela over to the South African security branch. We gave them every detail, what he would be wearing, the time of day, just where he would be."

The Associated Press went further the next day, naming Paul Eckel, then a senior CIA operative, as claiming Mandela's arrest "one of our greatest coups."

One of the countries that was receptive to backing the freedom struggle was not exactly free. East Germany saw apartheid as a reincarnation of Nazi-type fascism and was most helpful in educating ANC exiles, supporting the ANC's media outlets and printing *Sechaba* magazine. The South African Communist Party felt right at home, and Ahmed Kathrada, who would later be jailed with Mandela, went there for a World Young Congress that reinforced his commitment to nonracialism and internationalism.

IN 1963, in the heady aftermath of British Prime Minister Harold McMillan's famous speech about the "wind of change" sweeping through southern Africa, Joe Slovo, a Communist who was close to Mandela came to a politburo meeting in East Berlin and was asked by one of the "comrades" there how long he thought it would take to topple apartheid.

Ever eloquent, and a fearsome lawyer, Slovo had escaped from South Africa one step ahead of the security police. His wife, the journalist and activist Ruth First soon joined him with their children in London.

Now he was speaking to apparatchiks in an epicenter of the cold war. After citing various "forces and factors," and citing the anger and determination of the black people of his country, he guessed, "Six months."

Nearly thirty years later, he would be back in Berlin at what proved to be the last meeting of the party of the German Democratic Republic (GDR) as the Berlin Wall fell. An old man in the back of the room put his hand up after Slovo made his political report.

Slovo smiled as he told me the story in Johannesburg soon after he returned. "An older man with white hair waved his hand at me and said, 'Comrade Slovo, I am not sure if you remember me, but the last time you were here I asked you how long it would take to topple apartheid. What do you say now?'"

Slovo, wearing his trademark red socks, says he looked at the old man and recalled how optimistic he had been in his estimate back then. Then he added, "Yes, Comrade, I do remember your question, and I think I can say now what I said then: six months. I see no reason to revise my original estimate."

This time he was right.

OVER THE years, even as the Soviet Union and to a lesser degree China supported the ANC, support from another country—not widely known even in the movement—helped reorganize the ANC's army, Umkhonto we Sizwe.

That country was Vietnam. In the late 1970s, after the Vietnamese defeated the US and its South Vietnamese ally, an ANC "commission" went to Hanoi and met with, among others, their legendary General Giap. Fresh from winning their own liberation war, the Vietnamese provided strategic military counseling and support to the ANC, advising on the reorganization of their underground military units. The ANC published what they called "The Green Book" about the lessons learned from Vietnam.

The ANC also had many friends in Western countries, with Sweden perhaps the most generous and most supportive. When Sweden's Prime Minister Olof Palme was assassinated in 1986, suspicion quickly spread to South Africa's hit squads because of Palme's support for the ANC. A Swedish journalist wrote in 2013: "The case has never been solved and draws comparisons with the assassination of JFK for its notoriety and legion of conspiracy theories; 130 people have confessed to the murder, about 12,000 have been accused, and 450 possible murder weapons have been tested."

IN THE 1970s, as the external missions of the ANC and South Africa clashed, in the aftermath of the Soweto Uprising, another force emerged that was even more powerful, if less well organized, a global antiapartheid movement.

Ronnie Kasrils, a commander in the armed struggle for many years and later a minister in Madiba's, then Thabo Mbeki's, government, was very involved in organizing solidarity protests in the 1960s in London, where I was student, and was working with the ANC to infiltrate activists and later guerrillas into South Africa. He called the exercise "internationalism."

"We saw this in the international brigades in Spain, for example: physical volunteering to save the Spanish Republic from Franco, people coming from all countries. Britain, France, Germany itself, by the way, your country America. Some people from Africa and elsewhere. It's an understanding that when there's a fight for justice, wherever that's taking place, good people, people of conscience, need to stand up and raise up their voices and give their support. And so we saw the wonderful movement in the United States and then everywhere else for the Vietnamese people against the war of aggression, against Yankee Imperialism.

"The antiapartheid movement was a magnificent example of a worldwide movement in which solidarity played a very important part in shortening the days of apartheid rule."

Kasrils was involved in a special project over five years: to infiltrate students from Britain into South Africa to promote the ANC through underground work. I was one of the students who went there as part of the MK underground in 1967 as one of what are now called "the London Recruits."

He reminded me, "It wasn't just the protests, the demonstrations, the boycotts the sanctions and so on. . . . There's this book that's just come out, *The London Recruits*, about young people from Britain who I happened to meet, and others like a young guy from America or a young chap out of Greece, or his wife who happened to be from France, many young trade unionists, working-class people. Young communists, socialists of various shades, liberal-minded people who were actually prepared when we asked them to smuggle material into South Africa and did so. And that showed that generosity of spirit, and the fact that there are people who are always prepared to face danger for a just cause."

WHILE STUDENTS, young workers, and activists were responding on one side of the apartheid wars, the South African government sought out allies on the right. The government got involved in an "information" scandal, with pro-apartheid messages infiltrating the world's newspapers and being embedded into films. The government also bought weapons from, and collaborated on a nuclear program with, Israel.

When the economy was rocked after the Sharpeville massacre on March 21, 1960—during which scores of people were shot by police during an antiapartheid protest at a police station in the South African town of Sharpeville—many Western, especially American, companies poured in investment dollars to stabilize the situation. External investment in South Africa was considered to be very profitable.

Soon there was a global battle underway—in the media and in the streets, with South African agents launching its own external campaign, using a state-funded South Africa foundation to reach out to friendly elites and build support while also arming right-wing guerillas in Mozambique and Angola and then bombing ANC offices in Zambia and Zimbabwe. This struggle spread to other South African neighbors, then called "The Frontline States." I saw the damage as a producer of ABC News while filming a visit to Southern Africa by civil rights leader Jesse Jackson in 1986.

That was *their* "external mission."

A third force soon entered the fray, as Cuban military volunteers were sent back to Angola to confront the South Africans and their surrogates. Fidel Castro praised their intervention as an act of "proletarian internationalism."

The confrontation came to a head in the climactic battle in the town of Cuito Carnivale where the well-armed Cubans, with support from the Angolan army, stopped a South African advance. That led to negotiations, a Cuban and South African withdrawal from Angola, and soon, UN-fostered independence for Namibia which set the stage for the fall of apartheid.

Again, it was external forces that made the difference. Perhaps that's why Castro was cheered more loudly than any other head of state at Nelson Mandela's inauguration in 1994.

IT IS significant that soon after his release, Mandela left South Africa for an ANC conference in Lusaka, Zambia, where he was named Oliver Tambo's deputy president. From there, he began to tour African States, and in June visited eight cities in the United States. I made the film *Mandela in America* on that triumphant eleven-day tour with rallies and concerts in giant sports stadiums across the country.

Nominally, the effort was all about "thanking" supporters abroad, but in actual fact it was about fundraising for the election that was certain to occur. The ANC leader drew big crowds, but it's unclear how much money was raised by his inexperienced fund-raising machine, at least in the US. Mandela would later be criticized for taking money to support democracy from dictators and antidemocratic authoritarian states. But if he did so it was because the big corporate donors were still taking a wait-and-see approach.

Nonetheless, Mandela and the other leaders of the movement

recognized that the progress they made was not only the result of township uprisings and MK firefights but because of support in that "external world" that most white South Africans were unfamiliar with. By then, apartheid had become a global, not just a South African, issue, and it was world pressure that ultimately helped bring it to an end.

Rob Nixon wrote about South Africa in the American press and specifically about the cultural and media impact of Mandela mania. Nixon's writings on Mandela are discussed here by Jeanne M. Colleran in *Modern Fiction Studies*:

"Part of the appeal of South African cultural products internationally, and part of the reason for much of the uncritical reception extended them has to do with what Nixon rightly sees as a unique feature of South Africa's anticolonialist struggle: the extent to which the struggle became 'so fully globalized.'"

Nixon saw, she added, "Nelson Mandela as an American media icon, [recognizing] the widening gulf between spectacular media politics and the more ambiguous realm of actual political work. His description of the relentless American desire to appropriate Mandela's radical politics and transform them into a more benign Martin-not-Malcolm version of race relations is a second persuasive example of the refusal of American cultural conglomerates to view the players involved in any political drama in anything but binary terms."

Brilliant!

YOUTH

CHILDREN BORN in South Africa in the post-apartheid era are called "born frees." Some are very aware of the history that preceded them, while others do not connect to it at all.

The Root magazine reported: "The 'biggest challenge' for this maturing democracy is how it deals with the 'born frees,' says the Rev. Frank Chikane."

My Jet Online added:

> Without the struggles for political freedom, speech and equality, it has sometimes been said that the "youth of today" are more concerned about TV, clothes and social status than about acting upon and actioning their rights. It is true that many born frees have been granted access to more than even their older siblings have, such as being able to attend better schools and improved education. And yes, they probably do have access to more than previous generations.
>
> But what the born frees face is a different challenge—a challenge that will see them fighting against rampant crime, drug and alcohol abuse plus HIV/AIDS. These and other challenges they face will see them searching for leaders, role models and positive influences. It is therefore up to the leaders of today, parents, teachers,

government officials and all adults to guide young people and give them something to aspire towards so that they can take advantage of the world they find themselves in.

Mandela has written about his own upbringing in detail, his childhood in the Eastern Cape, the loss of his father, the stick games he played, his circumcision ceremony, and interactions he had with the regent, an official who was assigned to raise him, and whom he served loyally, even ironing his clothes before his real schooling began.

He was brought up in a traditional culture, one of thirteen children, and had three elder brothers all of whom were of higher "rank" in the Thembu hierarchy. When Nelson Mandela's father died in 1930, the paramount chief, Jongintaba Dalindyebo, became his guardian.

When he left his small community, he went to Johannesburg.

According to one of his biographers, Fatima Meer, he became imbued with the urban culture of the era—not just the politics—and was immersed in the music and arts of the vibrant scene in Johannesburg in the 1940s and '50s.

Yet his feelings about his childhood stayed with him in later life, especially after he was cut off from his own children. His own children in some cases grew resentful because as he became the father of the nation, he couldn't always father them in the ways he or they wanted.

The Daily Mail told the story of his first daughter:

It's perhaps no surprise then that to his close family, the cuddly, charismatic image built around him is frequently at odds with the introspective, emotionally aloof and patriarchal man they know.

Mandela's oldest surviving child is Dr. Makaziwe Mandela, known as Maki, his daughter from a troubled first marriage to nurse Evelyn Mase. And although she is now at peace with her father, she says that she struggled for years with feelings of anger and abandonment and that her older brothers Thembi (who died in a car crash in 1969) and Makgatho (who died of an AIDS-related illness in 2005) felt very much the same.

In her first major newspaper interview, Maki says: "As a child, before my father went to prison, I yearned to have both of my parents in my life, but it was my mother who brought me up. I had a father who had been there but not really there. He was not available to us."

Ironically, his first immersion in the struggle was as part of, then a leader of, the ANC's Youth League, which he pushed in a more militant direction. Later, I was with him when he said listening to youth movements is key to "helping us know if we are moving too slowly or too quickly."

When he set up foundations after his years in office, serving youth was a main focus. His principal foundation ran workshops with kids to dampen youth violence and better to key into how the generation thinks about itself and its future.

He also set up a Children's Fund, whose work is very close to Nelson Mandela's heart: "[ours is a] desire to make society more familiar with the smiles of children rather than their tears. . . . If this were true in our society, our youth would be happier, our communities safer, and our government reasonably at peace with its citizens."

Even as his charities serve and promote children's needs, many South African youth are conflicted about the importance of learning about the past. Many are more drawn to a US-style TV-spawned popular culture than political activism.

I spoke with Phumzile Manana, a researcher on the *Long Walk to Freedom* film. She was then involved in burrowing into the past to dig out historical detail, like when prisoners first wore sunglasses on Robben Island. While she has learned a great deal, she feels many in her generation no longer care.

"I don't think it's that people don't know. I just think it's come to the point where they don't care. Mostly the general consensus is, 'So what? Let it go. It's over now. It doesn't affect us. We weren't there for it.' So for them it means nothing, because they don't have to fight for anything. Everything has already been done for us. And that's just how it is these days. But that's not to say that they don't regard it as something important, it just doesn't affect them anymore."

"I mean, that's pretty cynical," I said to Phumzile Manana.

"That's how it is."

"Are you cynical?"

"I think I'm a realist. So you have to, before you can just ask a question like that, you have to look at the attitude of our parents as well. I mean, from the white side you could look at white guilt. We don't speak about it but it does exist. But white guilt can't exist without a counterbalance. And I think, for me, that would be black resentment. And that comes from our parents, and it filters down through the generations, so instead of having to deal with it yourself, you'd rather just ignore it, and pretend it isn't there. So by pretending it isn't there you just kind of shun apartheid. 'It's over, so what.' That's the feeling that I get from my friends, my generation."

"Then what's the meaning of this movie?" I prodded. "Why work on it? Why is it important? Why not just forget the whole thing? You know there have been a lot of TV shows about all this, why do we need this movie on top of everything else?"

"Because it's [still] our history! You can't move forward without your history. You have to place some importance on it, it has to be remembered. You can't just know about someone and have an idea of why they're important. You have to take it and you have to explore it. And then let it go and then move on from there. I think this movie is important as a way of bringing our country together. I'm not saying that we are divided—perhaps slightly. There are smaller groups that are. But this is like the bow that ties it all together."

ZUID-AFRIKA TO .ZA

THE PEOPLE who work with Mandela say he is constantly encouraging them to speak their mind, and to be critical when necessary. He has often criticized himself. I've quoted Mandela and others to the effect that he is not a saint or a savior. He was able to do what he did because so many "ordinary" people made extraordinary sacrifices alongside him, and even gave their lives for the noble idea that he and they fought for: freedom.

In our world—in these times of global terror and economic collapse—there are few stories that compare to the victory he achieved, and the warm feelings he inspired by his stoic focus on a better future for his people. How many leaders went from prison to president in our lifetime, and left office more respected and appreciated than ever?

In an analysis of the media and Mandela's messianism, Rob Nixon wrote:

> During his 27½ years of imprisoned fame, Mandela accrued a reputation of near messianic dimensions. There are several reasons for this: the redoubtable convictions of the man himself; the scale and inventiveness of the international tributes enacted in his name; the peculiar progress of his relation to the media; and the sweeping power, in South African history, of the idiom

and psychology of redemptive politics—deliverance from bondage, covenants, chosen people, divine election, promised lands, eschatologies, chiliasm, and apocalypse.

If these conditions have indeed generated a redemptive vision of Mandela, it is cardinally important to keep in view his efforts to repudiate the idolatry that accompanies messianic politics and can ultimately invite autocracy. From the instant of his release, Mandela has striven to dismantle the cult of personality constructed by the media and to subordinate his prestige to that of the ANC. We should concern ourselves therefore both with the cultural production of the messianic Mandela and with the limitations of redemptive politics.

To Pallo Jordan, the ANC veteran who worked with Madiba, and also quarreled with him (and was removed from a cabinet post because he frequently challenged the president, but was then brought back with a new portfolio), Mandela should be honored for what he did, not his larger-than-life image.

Jordan told us that Mandela is not a celebrity—even as many in the public, in the media, and in Hollywood say he is—but, nevertheless, "his contribution should be celebrated."

"I think that's an unfortunate dimension of a celebrity in the media, maybe the influence of Hollywood. But you find that everywhere," he said.

Celebrity is one problem, "deification" another, according to South African writer Zakes Mda. In his book, *Sometimes There is a Void*, he drew sharp reactions for criticizing Mandela for praising leaders in other African countries known as human rights abusers, and often rushing to the defense of comrades accused of wrongdoing.

"I went on to say that most of the problems we had in Africa began with the deification of our political leaders," he wrote. "They had fought for our liberation and as soon as they took over government we gave them such titles as the Messiah and the Redeemer. Why would they not have a Jesus complex?"

Mda then told of writing a long and very critical letter to Mandela. There was no written response, but, to his surprise, Mandela phoned him to set up a meeting with some of his cabinet members to hear the complaints. He treated them not as personal attacks but as an indictment of his organization.

Bill Bowles, who worked with the ANC in the early 1990s, told me Madiba always tried to be responsive, no matter who the critic was. "I was in the elevator once at Shell House, the ANC headquarters in Johannesburg, when the old man, as we called him, entered. A guy in the lift immediately started blasting him for the problems he was having finding a job. Mandela reached into one pocket for his notebook, and another for one of his no. 2 pencils, and asked the man his name and contact information. Then he promised someone would contact him. He was like that. I am sure someone did contact the man."

"I think Mandela does quite correctly insist that he be seen as part of this movement," explained Pallo Jordan. "And he always underscores that he never acted individually. He was always part of the collective, insisting 'the decisions I was involved in, and the actions I took, arose from collective decisions.' I think that's important."

Zelda La Grange, who worked for Mandela in the office of the presidency, confirmed that he was committed to working as a member of a group even after he was elected.

"All along there has never been any decision making where he was the only one doing it, or where he wanted to project to the world that he was the only one taking decisions. He will consult with all the people around him before taking any decisions and his office whether we take decisions, down to the smallest things like logistics. With everything there was always a consultative process."

I asked her if working with Mandela was like being in a "little democracy" within the bigger democracy.

"Yes, I think his office actually worked as a better democracy sometimes than the political democracy did. Democracy is part of the person he is."

THE LATE professor and public intellectual Jakes Gerwel, who was also Mandela's former cabinet secretary, also offered insights into Mandela's leadership style in "Living Out Our Differences: Reflections on Mandela, Marx and My Country—An Interview with Jakes Gerwel" by John Higgins, published in the journal *Thesis Eleven*:

> Mandela is a leader who throws up epistemological questions.
>
> We all cherish him and lionize him as this leader— which he really was—but he himself had a sense of collective leadership. He always raised the issue of how does the individual relate to the collective, how is the individual's experience and conduct influenced by the collective and how does it feed back to the collective?

What I remember most of all about Mandela as a decision maker was his ability to project himself from the present, the moment he had to make a decision, into the future, almost being able to stand at that future point and look back on the effect of a decision.

Added Pallo Jordan, "Of course in those political decisions, he might have had a particular role, but they were decisions of the collective. And I think that too is something that needs to be constantly underlined. Because I think it also is a lesson, not only about Mandela, but also about an ethic of the ANC, an ethic of collective leadership that you don't have 'presidentalism.'

"He never insisted that he was an infallible leader who was always right or that we must always follow him.

"Perhaps that is one of his great virtues, that some people attributed to years of introspection on the island. I don't think it's that so much. I think it's probably a quality he always had. It might have been particularly intensified during his time, the incarceration. You have a lot of time to yourself and you can introspect a lot.

"One of the difficulties I think that he confronted, and many of us confronted as well, was that Mandela [was] coming out [of] prison into a national executive, with most of the members of that national executive being my age group and my peers. The ethic of the ANC is [that] the president is first among equals. But Mandela was not actually among equals—he was among people who were his juniors, both in age and in terms of our memory of the movement as well.

"The closest person to his age in the national executive was someone like Joe Slovo. But the rest of the people were people who had come into the movement with the generation after Mandela. So he was not with his equals. He was, in a sense, head and shoulders above everyone. That of course complicated the situation greatly. Because there was the temptation on the part of many people to be reverential, to discuss who was first and not among his equals. And then of course there were others who insisted on the old ethic of first among equals. That, you know, creates tensions."

TREVOR MANUEL told us about one of those tense moments to offer insight into how Mandela acted and thought:

"Look, there were so many issues, but he would prod very hard, you know," he explained.

"One of the things he would say is, 'Boy, I want you to think with your head not your blood,' and that was frequently because he didn't want us to be angry, but against that he had certain ideas, one of the ideas he had was that the ANC should have some kind of a federal structure where all ethnic groups were represented on the national executive, and he would lobby. He would lobby, and before a meeting he would call everybody individually on the telephone, no cell phones, call us and try and lobby.

"There was a meeting where he wanted this line through, and the first person who opposed the view was Ahmed Kathrada and then we kind of all came in and Madiba banged the table—it was one time I saw him bang the table—and he kind of said, 'It's your organization, it's in tatters, you will destroy it, but it's yours. Destroy it.' . . . I think that having lived that close to him, you began to understand the qualities of leadership he lived, truly remarkably."

Those "remarkable" qualities elevated him to iconic status, but also left him open to political and commercial exploitation.

When he went into the hospital early in 2013, South African President Zuma's office seized control of the information coming out about his condition, wresting it away from his family. In the first of three hospital visits for a respiratory ailment, the president's spokesman, in a perception management exercise, minimized the seriousness of his condition at first, but then acknowledged the problems were more complicated, as was evident when he had to return twice more for medical treatments.

In late April 2013, President Zuma and colleagues staged a photo-op at the hospital in Pretoria for TV cameras from the South African Broadcasting Corporation (SABC) who then claimed an "exclusive." The problem was that Mandela seemed out of it, and uncomfortable, leading to a public outcry charging that he was being used, against his will, for political purposes.

Writing in the *Mail & Guardian*, Moshe Matheolane argued that his image was abused and his privacy violated:

[I]f only he could get the break that his retirement from public life and politics promised.

Unfortunately his name keeps getting pulled into publicity stunts, from politicians proclaiming in opportunistic eagerness that "Madiba is ours. He is our icon. He belongs to the ANC," to reality shows which quite frankly have very little if anything do with him, Madiba has been reduced to being nothing more than a political and commercial gimmick. It is in this light that it should come as no surprise that the latest ANC stunt in the

form of President Jacob Zuma's photo opportunity with
Madiba received the outrage that it did.

On America's National Public Radio, host Ashraf Garda
reported on the Media@SAfm show: "For many South Africans,
the coverage of his recent hospitalization and poor health seems
like media overkill. Older South Africans stress that the African way of coping with the twilight years is culturally nuanced.
It should be viewed as a final journey, and journalists should be
more sensitive to these customs."

And when the subject is raised in the context of his possible
death, Garda continued, "We get people who will call . . . to say,
'We don't speak about it, certainly not in our culture, not in black
culture, not in African culture.'"

In its coverage, a May 2013 article in the *New York Times* raised
other issues, writing,

> As Mr. Mandela fades away, the struggle to claim his leg-
> acy, his image, his moneymaking potential and even the
> time he has remaining has begun in earnest.
>
> The governing African National Congress, which Mr.
> Mandela led for decades, has been accused of using him
> as a prop to remind voters of the party's noble roots at
> a time when it has come to be seen as a collection of
> corrupt, self-serving elites. The party's main rival, the
> Democratic Alliance, has come under fire, too, for using
> a photo of him embracing one of its white progenitors,
> spurring complaints that the opposition is trying to
> co-opt Mr. Mandela's image to unseat his own party.

The Guardian's reporting on the issue charges that the unseemly fighting over money in the family goes back to 2005, when Mandela was told that some of his family trust documents had been altered without his consent, and that he was shocked when he learned that his daughters were trying to steer more money their way. He told them not to interfere with his efforts to provide funds for his extended family.

The newspaper referenced a document by Mandela lawyer Bally Chuene:

> Recalling Mandela's reaction when he found out, Chuene states: "Mr. Mandela was shocked and used a common expression, 'Good Lord.'" He was most infuriated and wanted to know when this had happened. He assured me that no such decision or approval had been given by him.
>
> Mandela called a meeting at his Johannesburg home in April 2005. Makaziwe and Zenani as well as Bizos and Mandela's wife, Graça Machel, attended. "During this meeting, Mr. Mandela made it clear to the applicants that he did not want them involved in his affairs," Chuene continues. "Mr. Mandela wanted the applicants to resign their trusteeships."
>
> Chuene accuses Mandela's estranged lawyer, Ismail Ayob, of colluding with Makaziwe and Zenani. Mandela "had become concerned that artworks were being sold, ostensibly on his behalf, without his authority or permission," Chuene said.

When he was in office, Mandela could be impatient and grumpy not only with his family but with his staffers as well, often seeking to cut off debate on economic policy and other issues. Former intelligence minister Ronnie Kasrils told me that when the government announced the Growth, Employment, and Redistribution (GEAR) economic strategy, ANC policymakers were shocked to be told it was "not negotiable." The policy later fizzled.

He also had a strong sense of vanity, according to Verne Harris of the Centre of Memory, and, so, was responsive when prominent people sucked up to him with effusive praises while seeking favors or support for their needs.

He was often driven by a sense of deep courtesy and sense of patronage in the Victorian sense, an approach that was key to the way he conducted himself, and so, for some who doted on him, he became an easy mark to be taken advantage of.

Those are also qualities he shares with millions of South Africans raised in a deeply religious and tribal culture that prizes deference to elders.

According to his former cabinet secretary, the late Jakes Gerwel, he had a deep affinity for ordinary people. "He had a genuine belief, and we often argued about whether or not this could be proved, that human beings are essentially beings who do good. He really acted on that. He is not naïve, but he has faith in the goodness of human beings, no matter how they disagree politically or otherwise, and he always acted in line with that belief."

JOURNALIST and archivist Padraig O'Malley said in a lecture at the University of Massachusetts in the fall of 1998: "If one were to finger the greatest failure of the Mandela years, it would perhaps come down to something very simple: The ANC simply underestimated the task it faced, indeed, the nature and dimensions of the task itself, and was unable to deliver on the promises it had made to the people. . . . As a result many blacks became disappointed with the government, and in time that disappointment turned to disillusionment."

In a cover story on Mandela's legacy, the *New African* wrote in July 2013 that "despite his socialist beliefs Mandela nationalized nothing during his presidency, fearing that this would scare away foreign investors. That decision was in part influenced by the collapse of the Soviet Union and the Eastern Bloc during the early 1990s and China's adoption of free market policies."

Many veteran ANC activists have misgivings that they rarely articulate for fear of being called disloyal. Retired speaker of the parliament Frene Ginewala, who was a tireless part of the liberation struggle, mused to me about her worries: "What worries me is the growing poverty. I look at the shantytowns, and I wonder, 'Is this what we fought for? Could we not have done better?' Secondly, I worry about the ANC. I worry about the values of all of us. What happened to our values? Have we lost our way? I do question, I think I've reached an age where I can question. I'm not blaming anybody. But I believe very strongly that we need a national value system."

PERHAPS THAT'S why so many people in South Africa admire him as a person who "represents the best in all of us," according to Father Michael Lapsley, a priest who served as chaplain for the ANC in exile until the apartheid security police sent him a letter bomb that claimed both of his arms, leaving him today with two hook-like prosthetic devices instead.

"Whenever, he went into the hospital, the whole country took a deep breath and exhaled a deep sigh of anxiety," says the man who is known as 'Father Michael': "We all are proud of how he led us."

He told me that Mandela uniquely understood the desires and needs of blacks as well as the fears of whites—and why they need each other. In short, he had a sense of the national psychology, not just its politics.

At the same time, writers like political scientist Tom Lodge found a calculated use of his personal "moral capital" as a tool for promoting political reforms. In his review of Lodge's work, Rob Skinner wrote,

> Using the concept of "moral capital," accumulated through leadership by example and the deliberate performance of actions that symbolize the aspirations of a wide constituency of followers, Lodge concludes with the suggestion that Mandela used such tactics to inspire an ideal of citizenship rather than to hold sway through popular adoration; and that his position as "democratic hero"—both within South Africa and worldwide—rested upon the extent to which his own personal experiences had become part of the public history.

There are always serious tensions and conflicts in politics, but Mandela's insight expressed in the phrase "no easy walk to freedom" put the challenge in perspective. There were always so many problems and dangers that might have derailed this process—and almost did. Mandela made choices and took risks throughout his life on issues and principles he believed in.

. . . Early in life, he could have been persuaded or been guilted into accepting an arranged marriage and staying in the Eastern Cape with some tribal leadership privileges.

. . . He was originally an African Nationalist. Had he not met Walter Sisulu, and been recruited into the ANC, he may have taken another path politically, or for that matter, taken none and spent his youth as a successful lawyer and an apolitical woman- izer even as he desperately sought the comforts of a family.

. . . He could have been killed when he was part of the armed struggle and was pursued and captured by the security police.

. . . His legal strategy at the Rivonia Trial, opposed at the time by all his lawyers, might have backfired, and he and his comrades could have been put to death.

. . . In prison, he could have succumbed to the harsh treat- ment or to depression. The unspoken secret of Robben Island is that some prisoners cracked. Physically, the tuberculosis he con- tracted because of the unhealthy prison conditions could easily have killed him and almost did.

. . . During Mandela's inauguration, we later learned, police dis- rupted an assassination plot by right-wingers. He was at risk—as was F. W. de Klerk, who tells me that his security force disrupted dangerous right-wing plots against him. On the nineteenth of December, 1992, de Klerk fired twenty-three senior officers he felt were scheming against him. The event became known as the "Night of the Generals." Both men lived in violent times, and many in South Africa still do.

None of these threats came to fruition. That doesn't mean

Mandela lived a charmed life, because in fact he seemed to have lived many lives, from herding cattle as a kid, to studying law, to becoming a lawyer, to creating a law firm, to joining the ANC and becoming part of its rebellious Youth League that propelled him into leadership, to moving a nonviolent movement into an armed struggle, just to name a few.

At every point, he showed himself to be ready to walk on the dangerous side of the road but did manage to survive despite the odds, though without diminishing the danger. He spoke out against corruption. He said, "It was such a sad disappointment to note that our own people who are there to wipe out corruption themselves become corrupt."

THESE ARE some of the reasons why the world deserves to get to know this story in all its detail and complexity. The producers of *Long Walk to Freedom* believe the movie will connect audiences worldwide with his story with all of the dramatic power that movies at their best can do.

No one film can tell it all, nor should even aspire to. That's why filmmaking is an art, not a science. It is there to move audiences, to mesmerize them to empathize and to care, and, hopefully, also to seek out additional information as the producers hope this book and our documentary series will provide.

Nelson Mandela's life is not over as we write. The story of the long walk to freedom is still being written and lived despite enormous obstacles that continue to impose painful political and economic compromises and an uncertain future.

And what does his biographer, Anthony Sampson, say about Madiba's legacy? "It is easy to overestimate the importance of a living hero with a universal charisma on a stage whose bright lights can fade soon afterward. His biography in the end converged with his mythology; and it was his essential integrity more than his superhuman myth which gave his story its appeal across the world."

We asked a number of the people about the challenge ahead.

ANC leader and former cabinet minister Pallo Jordan: "As he says in his book, that he casts his eye over the distance he has traveled, he dare not linger because the long walk is not yet over. As you climb one hill, there are many more vistas before you. So, the long walk continues for South Africa as it continues for him. What that long walk entails now I think is precisely creating the environment in which South Africans can enjoy that better life that was promised in 1994."

Writer Njabulo Ndebele: "I think that the metaphor of the long walk is a very good one, even when it was created. It was a suggestion that the fight for freedom is not a short-term thing."

No, it's not. It never is. On this point, there seems to be widespread agreement. The fight Nelson Mandela fought continues and will last, as will his contributions, many lifetimes more. Hopefully, this man, this son of the soil as he is sometimes called, will continue to teach us by his example, flaws and all, and by how he lived.

Former political prisoner Denis Goldberg: "The last page of Nelson Mandela's autobiography, in a way, quotes . . . is it Emily Dickinson? 'There are miles to go before I sleep, miles to go before I sleep.' Where have we come from? Where are we going to? He says when he was released from prison, people said, 'Well now you're free.' And he said, 'No, we're free to be free.'"

CHRONOLOGY

THE MANDELA century begins six years before the man we came to call Madiba was born on July 18, 1918. The African National Congress (ANC) is established on January 8, 1912, in Bloemfontein, although key ANC leaders had met earlier in Harlem in New York. Nineteen hundred and twelve is also the year that America's National Association for the Advancement of Colored People (NAACP) is born.

It isn't called the ANC at first but the South African Natives National Congress, organized along the lines of the British Parliament, with an upper and lower house. In 1923, it becomes the ANC. It brings clans and tribes together.

South Africa and the world change in the aftermath of World War I. The Afrikaners under Barry Hertzog form the National Party and soon have a covey of elite politicians, activists, intellectuals, religious leaders, and the Afrikaner Broederbond.

It is under the English colonial rulers that the first race-based laws are passed, especially the Natives Land Act, forbidding Africans to own land.

While Mandela has a relatively carefree childhood in the rural Eastern Cape, the rest of the world is in turmoil with the rise of the Nazi Party and Italy's Fascists. The Communist Party becomes a force around the world, a world that will soon plunge into a Great Depression. Unemployment grows and poverty deepens in South Africa. Striking white workers are shot in 1921. Two years later, the Native Affairs Act, once again imposed by the English, limits African access to towns.

MANDELA LOSES his father at age twelve and is sent to live with the acting regent appointed to oversee the aba Thembu people. The regent, Nkosi Jongintaba Dalindyebo, takes charge of his upbringing in what's called "The Great Place" at Mqhezweni.

AT SIXTEEN, Mandela is circumsized and initiated into the Thembu clan. He is sent to the Clarkebury Boarding Institute and then Heraldtown through high school.

IN 1939, the year that WW II begins, he becomes a student at the University of Fort Hare and enters politics as a member of the student representative council.

WITH THE 1940S, Mandela is suspended for joining an on-campus boycott. In 1941, he rejects an arranged marriage and moves to Johannesburg, where his first job is as a night watchman at a mine. He meets Walter Sisulu, who gets him a job as a law clerk. A year later, he attends university. He graduates in 1943. The next year, he joins the ANC, soon helping to form a more militant Youth League to push the organization to be more aggressive in the fight for African rights.

IN 1944, he marries Evelyn Mase. They have four children and move to Orlando in the area that will become Soweto.

BY 1948, as the all-white National Party wins office and imposes its policy of apartheid, Mandela becomes the Youth League's national secretary and studies law.

WITH THE 1950S, forced removals begin imposing racial segregation under apartheid with the passage of the Group Areas Act. Mandela moves up in the Youth League to become its president in 1951.

THE NEXT YEAR, an all-volunteer Defiance Campaign of civil disobedience starts, with Mandela as its "volunteer in chief." He is arrested but given a suspended sentence. The same year, 1952, he also forms a law partnership with Oliver Tambo.

IN 1953, Mandela drafts what is called the "M Plan" for an ANC underground.

THE ANC organizes the Congress of the People and adopts the Freedom Charter in 1955. Mandela watches the proceedings from a nearby rooftop.

HE MEETS WINNIE in 1957 and falls in love.

HE AND EVELYN divorce in 1958, and marries Nomzano Winnie Madikizela a few months later.

HE IS ARRESTED and charged in what becomes known as the Treason Trial. He is acquitted in 1961.

PROTESTS GROW in the 1960s. Police kill sixty-nine Africans in Sharpeville in 1969. The government proclaims a state of emergency, detaining some 2000 activists, including Mandela. The ANC and its rival, the Pan Africanist Congress (PAC), are banned. An all-white referendum establishes the Republic of South Africa. Repression of freedom movements intensifies.

IN THE AFTERMATH of the Sharpeville massacre, Mandela is detained and imprisoned for six months without trial. In 1962, he leads the ANC to establish an armed wing, Umkhonto we Sizwe (MK), the Spear of the Nation. He slips out of South Africa to build support and for military training. When he returns, he is arrested after a tip by the United States' Central Intelligence Agency and/or British Intelligence. He is punished with a five-year sentence.

ON JULY 11, 1963, police raid MK's secret meeting place, a farm called Liliesleaf in Rivonia, outside of Johannesburg. Top leaders are arrested and stand trial for sabotage in 1964. Mandela, already in prison, is added to the Rivonia group. He gives his "I am prepared to die" speech. Several of the defendants are acquitted, but Mandela and the other leaders draw life sentences and are sent to Robben Island off the coast of Cape Town.

THE ANC has already set up bases and a headquarters in exile under the command of Mandela's law partner, Oliver Tambo. Activists from other countries are infiltrated into South Africa for covert actions while a global antiapartheid movement forms.

MAY 12, 1969, to September 14, 1970, Winnie Mandela endures her longest and most torturous period in detention.

IN 1975, Mandela begins writing his autobiography secretly in prison.

MASS PROTESTS erupt again in 1976, as students in Soweto rebel against forced instruction in the Afrikaans language. A black consciousness movement organizes under the leadership of Steve Biko, who is arrested and murdered by police in 1977.

MANDELA AND his closest comrades remain politically active to the extent they can while in prison.

IN 1982, he and some of his fellow ANC leaders are moved to Pollsmoor Prison.

IN 1985, State President P. W. Botha offers Mandela his freedom if he speaks out against violence. Mandela rejects the offer and calls on Botha to stop state violence.

ALSO IN 1985, Mandela undergoes surgery for an enlarged prostate.

AS THE ANC calls on activists to make South Africa ungovernable, protests erupt in townships, many violent. A new state of emergency is proclaimed as Mandela begins secret talks with government ministers and intelligence officials to prepare for political change. Other secret talks between ANC leaders and Afrikaner intellectuals and business leaders begin outside South Africa.

IN 1986, Bruce Springsteen's close friend and band mate Little Steven Van Zandt and producer Arthur Baker create, with 58 stars, "the Sun City Project" to support the cultural boycott of South Africa with a hit record, video, and documentary. In 1988, a twelve-hour, globally televised concert in London celebrates his birthday. (An even larger all-star concert at Wembley Arena will greet his release from prison in 1990.)

IN 1988, Mandela is back in hospital to fight tuberculosis that he contracted in prison. When he gets out, he is moved to a house on the grounds of Victor Verster Prison in Paarl, an hour's drive from Cape Town. He continues having meetings with the government, as well as with members of his family and the ANC.

ON FEBRUARY 2, 1990, President F. W. de Klerk unbans the ANC and other political groups.

ON SUNDAY, FEBRUARY 11, 1990, Mandela is released from prison, walking free after twenty-seven-and-a-half years behind bars.

IN 1994, Mandela is elected president in the country's first non-racial democratic election. *Long Walk to Freedom* is published.

IN 1998, Mandela marries Graça Machel on his eightieth birthday.

IN 1999, he steps down as president after completing his five-year term.

ON JULY 18, 2013, he spends his birthday in hospital where his condition is diagnosed as "critical but stable." He has, against all odds, turned ninety-five. On September 1, 2013, he is discharged from hospital

NOVEMBER 2013. The film *Mandela: Long Walk to Freedom* is released.

POSTSCRIPT FOR "LEARNERS"

Six Lessons from Nelson Mandela

IN 2012, I spent part of Mandela's July 18th birthday, Mandela Day, in South Africa, at a big high school outside of Cape Town. Hundreds of students—called "learners" in South Africa—gathered for an assembly in a packed exercise yard.

They began by singing the country's national anthem "Nkosi Sikelel iAfrika," a hauntingly beautiful hymn asking the Lord to "Bless Africa." It was banned during the freedom struggle, and when it was sung the singers always held a fist aloft to express their determination to end apartheid.

The version that was heard that morning was a new one ordered by Mandela himself, fusing the original African words with a passage from "Die Stem," the official national anthem when the Afrikaners ruled, and a third lyric in English underscoring that South Africa was now home for all national and racial groups.

The new anthem was a symbol of a post–1994 commitment to nonracialism and reconciliation. No longer does anyone wave fists aloft.

After the anthem, there was one more song: a spirited "Happy Birthday" to Mandela. The version the kids adopted was the one introduced by Stevie Wonder, in one of his efforts to promote Mabiba's freedom during the prison years.

It wasn't clear to me if the kids knew the song's origins. If they didn't, it showed how seamlessly they had adopted the popular culture of an antiapartheid movement with a global footprint. That song travelled smoothly from Stevie Wonder's studio in Hollywood to their school in the Cape Flats. The blind musician, first known as "Little Stevie Wonder," clearly felt the connection between South Africa's history and heritage and his own, even as Nelson Mandela's ANC had its origins in Harlem in New York City, where the organization was born exactly a hundred years earlier, in 1912, the same year that American blacks founded the National Association For the Advancement of Colored People (NAACP), with similar goals to the ANC's.

After I filmed the enthusiastic, upbeat songs, I asked a few why they praised Mandela so effusively.

One told me how Mandela had "suffered and sacrificed" for South Africa. Others repeated that he had brought them "freedom," although it wasn't clear how they defined that, given they were attending an overcrowded, all-black school in a very poor township.

Most spoke of him as they might speak of superheroes they saw on television or at the movies—if they went to any. It was as if he had used a magic wand or superpowers to single-handedly throw off the yoke of oppression and lead South Africa, Jesus-like, to the promised land.

Mandela himself would enjoy their energy and adulation, but he would also try to tell them that he had not acted alone, that he was not Superman.

Students—learners—who get to see the *Mandela: Long Walk To Freedom* movie, or read this book and Mandela's autobiography of the same name will come to appreciate how long the struggle took, and how many obstacles had to be overcome. They will learn about people of different races and backgrounds who stood up for freedom and about the many who were beaten back, imprisoned, sometimes tortured and killed. They will see a whole history unfold—unfortunately a history that is not always well taught in their schools or in a culture that in its insistence to move forward all too often passes over the experiences of so many who gave so much for the new South Africa they are inheriting.

I like to think of six lessons I have learned from Madiba.

The movie tells Madiba's story on a political and personal level. It shows how he went from a rural area to attend school, and then university and law school. It shows how as a lawyer he fought for clients who were mistreated and deprived of their rights. You see how even as he became a leader he realized that he could never be free until his country was. That is the *first lesson*: We are connected to others and their needs are as important as our own.

He then discovered that he personally could not bring about the changes that he realized were necessary. There is a scene in the film where Mandela and his friends—Oliver Tambo, Walter Sisulu, Ahmad Kathrada, and others say that to make a fist you need many fingers, and to build a movement you need many people. That's the *second lesson*—the need for collective action, not just individual protest.

The *third lesson* is that you can't win unless you reach out to others, to like-minded Indians, whites, and Afrikaners. The movement became like an army when others realized the value of working together in alliances across racial and religious lines.

He then realized that you have to understand your enemies if you hope to overcome them. Madiba's *fourth lesson* was that he had to learn to speak Afrikaans, and win over people who feared him.

The *fifth lesson* was that the movement had to be flexible and people had to learn by doing. That meant making mistakes and learning from them. The movement went from nonviolence to violence, from community organizing to educating comrades in prison. (That's why Robben Island came to be called "Robben Island University.") He was diplomatic when diplomacy was needed, and militant when an armed struggle was required to defend the people.

He realized that South Africans couldn't win their freedom by themselves because Apartheid was such a powerful system. That's why he and the ANC reached out to friends and foes, to the United Nations, and other South Africans, Africans and people of the world to support the struggle.

Even as the apartheid South African government tried to isolate them by throwing activists in jail, he and his comrades isolated the government with boycotts and sanctions that forced the all-white ruling party to negotiate, to free prisoners and, ultimately, to end Apartheid This *sixth lesson* was decisive: You need to pressure your enemies by every means possible.

Those are the six lessons Madiba taught me. When you ask yourself what you would have done under the circumstances, what list do you come up with?

Would you have had the courage to stand up as Mandela and

his comrades stood up, to take personal risks for freedom, or would you have stayed on the sidelines and only worried about yourself?

Delving into this fascinating history can help you appreciate your own past.

Madiba has had a long life. If you asked him when he was your age if he believed he might spend much of his adult life in prison, and then go from prisoner to president, he would have laughed at you. It would have seemed so preposterous, an impossible nightmare, an impossible dream.

Danny Schechter
August 20, 2013

FURTHER READING

Nelson Mandela, *Long Walk to Freedom*

Nelson Mandela, *The Illustrated Long Walk to Freedom*

William Nicholson, *Long Walk to Freedom Screenplay*

Nelson Mandela, *Conversations With Myself*

Nelson Mandela By Himself: The Authorized Book of Quotations

Nelson Mandela, *The Authorized Comic Book*

Nelson Mandela: The Authorized Portrait

Anthony Sampson, *Mandela: The Authorized Biography*

Fatima Meer, *Higher Than Hope, An Authorized Biography*

Elleker Boehmer, *Nelson Mandela*

Tom Lodge, *Mandela; A Critical Life*

Martin Meredith, *Nelson Mandela: A Biography*

Joseph Ajay Fashagaba, *The Life History of Nelson Mandela and South Africa*

Father Michael Lapsley, *Redeeming The Past*

Stephen M Davis, *Apartheid's Rebels*

Barbara Rogers, *White Wealth and Black Poverty*

Jay Naidoo, *Fighting For Justice*

Anthony Sampson, *Black and Gold Tycoons, Revolutionaries and Apartheid*

Denis Goldberg, *The Mission: A Life For Freedom in South Africa*

Patrick Bond, *Elite Transition*

Sampie Terreblanche, *Lost In Transformation*

Fran Buntman, *Robben Island and Prisoner Resistance to Apartheid.*

Zakes Mda, *Sometimes There is a Void*

William Gumede, *Restless Nation*

Stanley Greenberg, *Race and State in Capitalist Development*

Ronnie Kasrils, *Armed and Dangerous*

Ahmed Kathrada, *Memoirs*

Ken Keable, *London Recruits*

Joe Slovo, *An Unfinished Biography*

Firdoze Bulbulia and Fatth Isiakpere, *Council Of The Elders*

Eddie Daniels, *There and Back, Robben Island, 1964–1979*

Martin Plaut and Paul Holden, *Who Rules South Africa*

Alan Wieder, *Ruth First and Joe Slovo in the War Against Apartheid*

Jomarié Dick, *Viva Mr. Mandela*

David Goodman and Paul Weinberg, *Fault Lines: Journeys into the New South Africa*

ABOUT THE AUTHOR

DANNY SCHECHTER has produced and directed six documentary films about Nelson Mandela, including *Free At Last* (1990); *Mandela in America* (1990), with producer Anant Singh; *Countdown to Freedom: The Ten Days that Changed South Africa* on the 1994 elections; *Prisoners of Hope* with Barbara Kopple on the reunion on Robben Island (1995); *A Hero for All* (1998); and served as a contributing director on *Viva Madiba*, marking Nelson Mandela's ninetieth birthday.

Danny was the only American documentary filmmaker Mandela trusted to be part of his team in the United States and in South Africa, time and again, for the last several decades since his release and his election as South Africa's president.

Danny Schechter was introduced to South Africa as a "London Recruit" for the ANC and MK in an illegal propaganda action in 1967. He organized the Africa Research Group in Boston and worked with Southern African liberation movements including the ANC. As a filmmaker and journalist, he created and produced *South Africa Now* for Globalvision. It was a weekly TV series uncovering uncensored news from South Africa that was broadcast on public television stations in the US and in more than thirty countries around the world for three years. (It was banned in South Africa.) He joined rock and roll musician Little Steven Van Zandt to organize the Sun City Anti-Apartheid Music Project. He later helped produce the globally televised Wembley Concert that welcomed Mandela to London.

Among Danny's books are *The More You Watch, The Less You Know*. He was an Emmy Award–winning producer for ABC News, and prior to that was known as "Danny Schechter the News Dissector" as news director on Boston's WBCN Radio. Later, he was a producer for CNN, ABC News and CNBC. He writes for AlJazeera.com and comments on BBC, Al Jazeera, and RT. Danny has just completed a three-hour TV series, *Inside Mandela: The Long Walk to Freedom: The Making and Meaning of Nelson Mandela's story.*

Danny Schechter blogs at newsdissector.net and edits MediaChannel.org and can be reached at dissector@mediachannel.org.

OTHER BOOKS BY DANNY SCHECHTER

Dissecting the News & Lighting the Fuse, NewsDissector.net, 2013

Blogothon, Cosimo Books, 2012

Occupy: Dissecting Occupy Wall Street, Cosimo Books, 2012, ColdType.Net (eBook)

The Crime of Our Time: Why Wall Street is Not Too Big to Jail, The Disinformation Company, 2010

Plunder: Investigating Our Economic Calamity, Cosimo Books, 2008

When News Lies: Media Complicity and the Iraq War, Select Books, 2006

The Death of Media and the Fight to Save Democracy, Melville House Publishing, 2005

Embedded: Weapons of Mass Deception (How the Media Failed to Cover the War on Iraq), Prometheus Books, 2003, ColdType.Net (eBook)

Media Wars: News at a Time of Terror, Rowman & Littlefield Publishers (USA), 2003, Innovation Books (Bonn, Germany), 2002

News Dissector: Passions Pieces and Polemics, Akashic Books, 2001, ElectronPress.com, 2000

Hail to the Thief: How the Media "Stole" the 2000 Presidential Election (Edited with Roland Schatz), Innovation Books, 2000, ElectronPress.com (USA)

Falun Gong's Challenge to China, Akashic Books, 1999, 2000

The More You Watch the Less You Know, Seven Stories Press, 1997, 1999

INDEX